MW01088143

THE UNKNOWN WITNESSES

THE UNKNOWN WITNESSES

By Colleen L. Reece

Reorganized Church of Jesus Christ of Latter Day Saints

Copyright © 1974
HERALD PUBLISHING HOUSE
Independence, Missouri

Library of Congress Catalog Card No. 73-87642
ISBN 0-8309-0107-8

All rights in this book reserved. No part of the text may
be reproduced in any form without written permission of
the publishers, except brief quotations used in connection
with reviews in magazines or newspapers.

Printed in the United States of America

DEDICATION

For Mom and Doug . . .
who believe in me

TABLE OF CONTENTS

PREFACE

One of the rich resources of our faith is in the testimony of personal experience. While many interpretations may be placed on particular experiences, those which bear the stamp of communion with God have in common the capacity to encourage both those who testify and those who receive the testimony.

Sister Reece's testimonial introduction quickens in us an appreciation for her treatment of the testimonies of persons whose names we do not know but whose experiences are recorded in the scriptures.

We trust that the Spirit of love and life will bless those who read.

THE FIRST PRESIDENCY

AUTHOR'S TESTIMONY

As you read these stories may the Spirit of God which prompted their writing also touch each of you.

God often uses us in ways we do not expect. For example, I have always hated getting up early. Yet throughout these last months I have awakened many times at 5:00 a.m., ready and alert to set down on paper the thoughts in my heart and mind.

May God bless each individual who seeks to become his witness. I thank him for the beautiful experience this writing has brought to me.

Colleen L. Reece

A MOTHER'S LOVE

I Kings 3:16-27: "Then came there two women, that were harlots, unto the king, and stood before him. . . . Then said the king, The one saith, This is my son that liveth, and thy son is the dead; and the other saith, Nay; but thy son is the dead, and my son is the living. . . . And the king said, Divide the living child in two, and give half to the one, and half to the other."

Last night I dreamed, as I have dreamed so many times in the past months, that I heard my baby cry. It was so real I awoke to find myself holding my little son close to my breast and whispering. "I will never let you go." He stirred a little in his sleep as the wave of terror within me receded once again.

I lay there sleepless, thinking over the dream, which was factual in every detail. Many years ago when I was still a young girl, my parents were forced to sell me as a slave in order to save the family from starvation. My master was kind, and soon I became one of his favorites, but when he died I was left alone, for he had made no provision for his slaves. I could not return to my parents, for the mistress of a wealthy landowner, even though she had been a slave with no choice in the matter, would be stoned to death by the people of the village.

There seemed no way left to me but death, yet I could not take my own life for now I knew that within me another life was being formed. I could not destroy my child although hope for me seemed gone.

A few months before the birth of my son I finally took the only step left to me and approached one who kept a house of pleasure for rich men who wanted to hire a woman. She felt sorry for me, I think, for she, too, was soon to bear a child. She told me I need not ply the trade until a proper amount of time had passed after my child was born. I was too weak and sick to care, or even to be grateful, but a determination had begun to grow within me to keep my child, no matter what I had to go through in order to do so.

At last the time of my deliverance came, and as my son was brought forth, wrapped, and placed in my arms, I rejoiced. Nothing could equal the feelings I had as I looked into his tiny face. He was strong, and healthy, and beautiful; he was someone I would protect with all the fierceness of a mother's love—he was mine.

Just three days after my son was born the other woman's son was delivered. He too was a beautiful child, but pale and thin, and he lay still and quiet while my son cried to be taken. The next morning I awoke and gazed in horror at the child at my bosom, for there lay the other woman's child, who had died in the night. My son was at her breast. I demanded that she return my child but she would not confess to changing the babies and refused to give him to me.

The great king Solomon was in the city that day so we took my son and sought audience with him. It was a long time before we could gain entrance, and as we were led through the long halls to his presence, I trembled with fear and weakness.

Is it hard to believe that even such as I could love a son so much? Many women in my position gave the children they bore to anyone who wanted them. I could hear my little son crying for me as I told the story in hesitant and fearful tones to the king. There were many in the palace that day, and as I spoke I saw the faces of those who watched. Some were hostile—what right had such as I to take up the king's time? Some looked bored—I was just another case to them. A very few seemed sympathetic.

When I had finished the other woman also spoke. She told the king I was a little unbalanced and perhaps didn't realize it was my son who had died, not hers. I could only brokenly reiterate that the living child was indeed my son. At last the king held up his hand.

"Bring me a sword," he said. And they brought a sword to the king. I can see it now, shining brightly in the dim courtroom, as he held it up and said, "Divide the living child in two, and give half to the one, and half to the other."

"No!" I screamed, and threw myself on the floor at the king's feet, "O my lord, give her the living child, and in no wise slay it!" My heart felt torn from its roots. My son—the only person on earth I loved—and now he too would be taken from me. Yet it was better to give him away and never see him again than to see him put to death.

As I lay prostrate at the king's feet I saw the triumphant gleam that came into the other woman's eyes as she cried, "Let it be neither mine nor thine, but divide it!" Was she mad? How could any sane woman stand there agreeing to such a proposition? I had never known such agony as I felt at that moment. A great silence fell upon the room. Then the king commanded me to rise, and he answered the unspoken question that trembled upon the lips of each one there.

"Give her the living child, and in no wise slay it; she is the mother thereof." As my little son was placed in my arms, a mighty and triumphant cheer arose in that courtroom for the wisdom of the king.

Clutching my baby I stumbled through the doorway and into the street. Unfamiliar words were coming from my mouth, words I had not used since childhood. "Oh, give thanks, praises be to Jehovah!" I did not know where I could go, but the Almighty One had given back my son. No longer would I walk in wicked ways even if I had to beg to feed and clothe my child.

As I stepped into the dusty road, a humble shopkeeper approached me. He was old and worn, yet in his face was a look of kindness. As he spoke, I felt he had been sent to me from Jehovah himself.

"My wife and I were in the courtroom," he said. "We are old, and have no children. Our daughter died when she was just about your age. We have little to offer, but you are welcome to what we have. We would like you and your son to become our family." His wife, a few steps behind him, held out her arms. Tears streamed down her cheeks and I ran into the shelter of those arms which reached out to us so lovingly. I felt as though I had at last come home.

So now, even though the dream comes again and again, I awaken to reality, with my son safely beside me. I give thanks each day for the hard work, the coarse food, and the rough shelter. But most of all I give thanks that I will be able to raise my son within this humble cottage where we dwell with the shopkeeper, his wife—and Jehovah.

THE BRAVE SERVANTS

II Kings 5:1: "Now Naaman, captain of the host of the king of Syria, was a great man with his master, and honorable, because by him the Lord had given deliverance unto Syria; he was also a mighty man in valor, but he was a leper."

There is a strange drawing power that attracts one to another. I feel this in our little maid, a captive Israelite who serves my wife. There is devotion in her service beyond understanding. She should hate us for taking her from her own land; instead she loves us. Her ways are gentle, and in spite of the shadow of sadness in her eyes, she is a merry child who often plays with my own children while my wife is resting. I can hear her low voice in the nursery telling stories of her country and her God—I believe Jehovah is his name.

My heart is indeed troubled, for today I noticed that the small white patch on my leg is growing. At first I had thought it was nothing, but now I must face the accursed truth the king's own physician

19

imparted—I am a leper! Yet it is impossible for me to accept this. Am I not Naaman, captain of the Syrian army? Am I not mighty and strong, and did not the Lord himself use me to deliver Syria? I have always tried to live honorably. Why should this living death fall on me?

How can I tell my wife? This last thought brings a white hot thrust of pain for I must go away and never see my family again in order to protect them. A bitterness fills my being at the irony of it all—protect them from me, the one who loves them more than life itself.

Pulling off my boots I once again examine that betraying piece of flesh, visualizing the day my body will be consumed by the dreadful disease. A slight rustling in the doorway causes me to look up. My beautiful wife stands there, a look of fear and compassion on her face. Her eyes are on the scaly white patch and at last she speaks, "What will you do?"

In amazement at her knowledge I question her further, to find that she has known for several days. The little serving maid noticed the patch the day I cut my foot and she so deftly bandaged the wound. At first she feared even to mention it to my wife. At last she knew she must, for within her heart was the belief that if I could only go to the prophet Elisha in Samaria, my leprosy would be taken away.

Such foolishness! Leprosy is incurable. In anger I call for the servant Gazi. He too had been brought to us from Israel. "Yes, such things have been known to happen. If my lord would go to Israel, it would hurt nothing and perhaps there would be a miracle; this man walks with God." As he finishes speaking a shaft of sunlight touches his strong face and my decision is made. I will go.

* * *

The next few weeks were busy ones as I made preparation for the trip. My beloved friend, the king of Syria, provided a bountiful offering for me to award the prophet in payment of the miracle, should I be healed.

When I at last arrived at the palace of Israel and presented my introductory letter to the king, he rent his clothes saying, "Am I God that the Syrian king has sent this man to me, that I might recover him of leprosy? He must again be seeking an argument, an excuse to start war."

My despair was mingled with black anger at the little maid and Gazi, for on the journey I had almost been persuaded to believe it might really happen. Was this their revenge on me for capturing them?

21

Just then a king's messenger knocked at my door. "There is a man of God named Elisha," he said. "When he heard of you, he sent word to the king for you to come to him that it might be known unto you that there is a prophet in Israel."

Why not, I thought to myself. I had come this far; I might as well go see the man. If he were indeed a prophet perhaps he could call on his God that my leprosy be recovered.

When I came to his door and waited in my chariot the prophet did not appear. Instead he sent a cryptic message, telling me to go wash seven times in the Jordan River and I would be clean. In disbelief I sat there for a moment. If the situation had not been so tragic it would have been laughable. Wash in the Jordan and be clean? Why, it was the time of year when silt poured into the streams; anyone washing there would need a good scrubbing to remove the river's dirt from his person! If I must wash in a river it would be my own clean waters at home, not any of these filthy Israelite rivers!

I can never remember feeling such rage as I did at that moment. As Gazi came near me I raised my hand to strike him down. Fool I had been to believe a leper could be made clean, and this man had led me to utter despair and humiliation.

"My lord," he said, and something in his voice stayed my upraised hand, "you must not leave in anger. You must obey the prophet. If he had asked you to accomplish great tasks you would have done them no matter what the cost to yourself. Will you not then humble yourself and go wash as he has asked?"

My brain felt as though it would explode in its fury. How dared this traitor speak so to me? "Yes," I cried, "I will do as I have been told—I will dip into this filthy water seven times, but if I should come forth yet unclean, it will be your life that is required—yours and the little maid's!" Gazi's face paled but his look did not waver. "So be it," he quietly replied, and even in my wrath I wondered how anyone could have that much belief in an idea.

Throwing my tunic to the bank, I shuddered as I entered the brown, rolling waters. As they closed around me I gasped, holding my hand over my face to keep off some of the mud. Once, twice, three times—I looked at my leg. Merciful God, the leprous patch was spreading! Four times, five times, six times I dipped into the water. By now my whole leg was white and the strength was draining from me. If I had not given my word to Gazi, even now held captive by two of my men, I would never have had the strength to enter that filthy stream for the seventh time. My hate sustained me and I hobbled once again into the murky depths. A burning sensation filled my body and, knowing it was the end, I forced myself under the water where my men would not see my last futile effort.

Suddenly with a great surge of feeling my mind cleared. My body seemed strong, stronger than ever before, and with a loud cry I ran from those muddy waters and threw myself at Gazi's feet. "I am clean," I shouted, and the sound rang back from the heavens themselves. "Praises to Jehovah, I am clean!" My body shone in the sunlight and the skin was fresh and firm as the flesh of a child. Gazi's eyes filled with tears as he embraced me, and a loud cheer came from the throats of my men, who had dropped to their knees on seeing me healed. "Oh, Master, I rejoice with you. I knew if you would only do it God's way, as he asked, you would be healed." I realized the bravery both he and the faithful little serving maid had exhibited. They were so sure I would be healed if I would only humble myself.

When we returned to Elisha's door, he stood there smiling, yet he would take no reward for my healing. I told him I knew now that there was only one true God and he was the God of Israel. Never again would I praise or make sacrifices to any god but Jehovah, and the selfless devotion of my servants would be rewarded.

"Go in peace," Elisha said, and with this benediction we started our journey home. Home! What a beautiful sound . . . for now I had not only strength and health to offer my family but the strength of the Lord God of Israel—and all because of the faith of Gazi and the little maid who loved me enough to risk their lives to save mine.

THE FIRST MIRACLE

John 2:1-10: "And on the third day of the week, there was a marriage in Cana of Galilee; and the mother of Jesus was there. And Jesus was called, and his disciples, to the marriage."

I awakened early this morning long before it was light. All the world was quiet and still as I lay for a moment thinking of the day to come. Suddenly the silence was broken by a little bird whose throat seemed to be splitting from the song he was pouring forth. How beautiful—and how fitting—for today was my wedding day.

The words repeated themselves in my mind and the image of my beloved arose before me: Joel, strong and handsome, yet so gentle and kind. Tears of joy welled up in my eyes and I felt like raising my voice with that of the little bird. It was good to have these moments alone. Our households had been busy for days preparing for the marriage. Joel had the wine ready for opening, we had the cakes baked, my dress was finished, and today was the day!

This day seemed long in coming to a small girl who had idolized Joel for so many years. He was my hero. I must confess that through the years he treated me as a little sister but at the marriage of my friend Joanna he suddenly looked at me with new eyes. Perhaps it was the long white gown or my hair piled high on my head for the first time. Something made a difference. In the days to come the courtship proceeded according to custom until all arrangements had been made. My parents were well pleased, and the moments Joel and I had together were pure joy. Now our wedding day was here. I prayed in my heart that the day might be perfect and the memory cherished forever.

Strange as it now seems the hours sped by. The day was sunny, all I had hoped for, and at last Joel and I were standing in front of the banked flowers the servants had so lovingly placed. My long dress covered the slight trembling of my knees as the benediction of peace was pronounced.

So many guests had come! There was Martha, and Johnathan, and, oh, yes, my friend Mary of Nazareth and her son Jesus, with some of his companions. As Joel and I made our way through the people, greeting them and making them welcome, I was filled with pride in my new husband and happiness that so many had come.

My mother beckoned me, and whispered, "The wine is all gone."

Hastily I reported this to Joel who followed me to one side. "How can this be?" he asked. "We prepared so carefully!"

"The day has been warm," Mother replied, "and the people are many. What shall we do?"

What indeed! There seemed to be nothing we could do.

In the doorway I could see Mary of Nazareth—Mary, to whom I had poured out my childish troubles many times. Instinctively I ran to her, my eyes filling with tears, and told her what had happened.

"There, child," she comforted me, "do not grieve. We will see what can be done." And turning to her son Jesus she said, "They have no more wine."

His kind eyes looked at me in my bridal finery, then back to his mother. "What will you have me do? That will I do; for my hour has not yet come."

Quickly calling the helpless servants Mary told them to follow the directions her son would give.

In one end of the kitchen there were six large stone water pots. Jesus asked the servants to fill them all with clean, fresh water. As they were filled to the brim our humiliation grew. Not to have enough wine for our guests was unthinkable, yet we would have to finish serving them with water. My wedding day was ruined.

Quietly Jesus asked the servants to draw a cup from the water pot and take it into the feast governor. In spite of my feelings I choked back the tears and slipped into the corner of the room as he drank from the cup. Shaking his head as though he could not believe it, he called out, "Joel!"

I could see the little frown that crossed his face, for a strange tone was in the governor's voice. As Joel reached him, the governor clapped him on the back and laughed. "You have played a trick on us, clever one! Every other man I know sets forth the good wine first; then, after all have drunk, he serves the poorer quality. But you," and his enormous frame shook with his mirth, "you have saved the best wine until last!"

Joel smiled at the governor. "Let us see for ourselves," he said.

The servants poured us a cup of the wine from the stone jars that had so recently been filled with water and we raised them to our lips. Never had we tasted such smoothness. The wine was fresh and clean, clear as the tang of grapes with early morning dew yet on them.

"Come," Joel said, and grasped my arm, "we

must find Jesus and thank him." We searched throughout the house but he was nowhere to be found. One of the servants told us he and Mary had just gone out. Hastening to the doorway we saw him some distance away, his mother's hand upon his arm. In silence we watched as evening shadows surrounded them, then turned to each other.

"We must thank him later," Joel said earnestly. "It was a miracle, you know." He hesitated, then continued, "Somehow it didn't seem fitting to run after him at this moment."

"I know," I replied softly, and my eyes were on those distant figures, now almost out of sight. "There was a strangeness about him, as if he came to our wedding a boy but left it as a man."

Joel's hand tightened on mine. As we gazed into the distance I knew he understood. No longer was Jesus visible on that dusty road, yet I felt that our wedding day at Cana had been a beginning, not only for Joel and me but for the carpenter's son as well.

A CENTURION'S FAITH

Matthew 8:5-13: "And when Jesus was entered into Capernaum, there came unto him a centurion, beseeching him, and saying, Lord, my servant lieth at home sick of the palsy, grievously tormented."

I waited anxiously outside old Ebed's door as the doctor's footsteps drew nearer. When he came out his face was lined with the efforts he had made, and I knew before he spoke that those efforts had been unsuccessful.

"He is resting a little more comfortably," he told me. Then sadly shaking his head, he said, "There is nothing more I can do." Quickly he turned away from the stricken look I knew had come to my face.

I gazed at him unseeing, for in memory I had returned to the past, to that day thirty or more years before when Ebed had come to tell me my father was dead. "You must be brave," he said, "for you must take care of your mother and little sister." I could never forget the years following, for it was he rather than I who watched over and cared

31

for our little family. When I grew older I offered him his freedom but he smiled and said gently, "Master, where would I go? I have no one; you and your family are the ones I live for. My bonds of service are the chains of love." We never discussed freedom after that, and he continued to look after us.

Now Ebed was old and sick. I had accumulated enough for us to live comfortably and was gaining popularity with the ranks I commanded. Was there no way I could repay Ebed's faithful devotion?

I entered his little white room, sparsely furnished in spite of my protests, for he wanted no luxuries. Hot tears filled my eyes as I gazed at this faithful friend. Through the years he had come to fill the place of my father. His body was shaking with palsy, and he could not rest.

I turned to go but he cried out, "Master!"

I knelt by his bedside, taking his poor gnarled hand in my strong ones. "What can I do?" I asked. His whisper barely reached me: "The Galilean."

I remembered then the strange stirrings in my heart when old Ebed had told me of the young prophet who taught from the mountaintop. It was said that he healed the sick and had compassion on the poor and lowly. I could not take my servant to him, but surely he would come.

"Yes, Ebed, I will go!" A look of radiance crossed his face even as another spasm left him shaking and weak once more. With a farewell clasp of his hand I hastened away to find the "Christ" as I had heard him called.

Happiness welled up inside me as I traveled the dusty roads in search of him. Incredible as it may seem, I did not doubt that I would find this Jesus and that he would heal my servant. Far ahead I could see a great crowd of people, and I began to run to join them.

At the city gates the multitude fell back at the sight of my Roman garb. In their eyes was amazement and unbelief. Why would a Roman centurion be seeking the Galilean? Was I coming to harm him? I saw uncertainty on their faces and heard frightened whispers, but since I was large of stature I made my way through the crowd and stood facing him, the one I sought.

I looked into his face. Involuntarily I snatched the helmet from my head and dropped to my knees. "Lord, [and as I called him that I knew it was true], my beloved friend and servant is home sick with palsy. He is faithful and kind, yet now he is tormented until my heart breaks to see him so."

Jesus placed his hand upon my shoulder and said, "I will come and heal him."

I knelt there before him and suddenly I felt that I too had been healed—healed of weaknesses within me I hadn't known were there. My ears could hear truth, and my voice spoke: "Lord, I am not worthy to have you come under my roof. If you will only speak the word, I know Ebed will be healed." I paused, then continued, "I too am a man under authority, and I have many soldiers under me. I tell men when to go and when to come, and I tell my servant what to do and he does it."

There was silence. Then Jesus turned and spoke to the crowd. He told the multitudes that he had not found such faith even in Israel. He spoke to them of Abraham, of Isaac and Jacob, then he turned to me. "Go thy way; as thou hast believed, so be it unto you."

The last rays of the setting sun were gilding the rooftops as I hurried home to my family, and there by the front gate was a figure clothed in light. A final beam of the setting sun surrounded my servant as he met and embraced me. No longer was he old Ebed, crippled and bent. Gone were the convulsions that racked his body. He stood straight and tall before me, a gloriously strong and healthy man.

"Just at the noonday hour," he said, with a look

on his face I could never describe, "a voice spoke, telling me to arise, and I became whole."

I remembered Jesus' words that my servant would be healed in the selfsame hour. My heart was filled with joy as we entered our home to tell the good news, not only of Ebed's healing but of mine—for which is greater, the healing of a body or the healing of a human heart? No longer would I be content merely to live from day to day. I must again seek and perhaps follow the Christ who had touched both Ebed and me.

SOMEONE TOUCHED ME

Mark 5:23: "And Jesus, immediately knowing in himself that virtue had gone out of him, turned him about in the press and said, Who touched my clothes? And his disciples said unto him, Thou seest the multitude thronging thee, and sayest thou, Who touched me? And he looked round about to see her that had done this thing."

In fear and trembling I knelt there before him, an island in the midst of the multitude. Looking into his face I whispered, "It was I, Lord!"

A little pool of silence greeted my statement and through my mind flashed all the years leading to this moment. It seemed so long ago, and indeed it had been long. Twelve years had passed since the physician had told me he could do no more; I had a rare disease which caused an issue of blood. In the endless months following, my world became comprised of hopeful visits to one physician, then another, and another; an endless stream of physicians examined me, shook their heads sadly,

36

and turned away. Always my family prayed I could be helped, but as the years passed hope seemed to sink low.

We had been a well-to-do family, but the physicians' fees were high, and now there was little left. Since the death of my parents my brother and I had lived in a small cottage on the edge of town. There was barely enough to cover even our simple needs. My beloved younger brother—the thought of him brought tears to my eyes. I could see him daily growing pale and thin from the effort of caring for me while he worked to support us. I knew he did not eat properly but saved the best for me, yet in spite of his sacrifices my condition was steadily worsening.

As I watched him the thought would rush through me, If only I were well and strong, I would care for him!

Perhaps it was this last thought that had given me strength this morning. When he had gone to work for the day, I had slowly crept from my bed, something I had been unable to accomplish for several weeks. What an effort it had been even to put on a simple dress. With shaking hands I had pulled a veil over my hair; I had no strength to arrange it. I had prayed in my heart that I might be able to do what I must do, for I had heard of a miracle man and I was determined to go to him.

Strangely enough, I never once doubted that he would heal me. I knew if I could but make my way to him the disease within my body would leave and I would be given peace.

Step by step I walked that long road from our door to where I could see him with his followers. He was surrounded by masses of people listening in awe to his words. Dismayed at the sight of the crowd, I sank to a stone for a little rest. How could I ask him to heal me? There were so many people, crowding and jostling for a better view of him— could I ever even get to him?

My efforts seemed to drain what little strength I had left, but he was my only chance for life; I had to reach him. I arose from my resting place. Inch by inch I worked my way toward him. Weakness poured over me, and just at the moment I knew I could go no farther, I came to the edge of the little group who encircled him.

There was a slight movement among his companions. Fearing that they might be preparing to leave, I slipped between two of his friends and for a moment grasped the rough cloth that was his cloak.

Within my body was a great upheaval. The blood in my veins stirred with life and my pulse grew steady. I could see health showing in the hands that had been white for so long. So happy was I at these discoveries that I had not sensed the stillness as Jesus turned to his disciples and asked who had touched his clothes. As they questioned his meaning, I fell before him. What had I done? I knew I had been healed, but now I must confess.

Again I said, a little more loudly this time, "It was I, Lord. For twelve years I have been growing steadily worse with this blood disease. No one could help me. I knew that if I could come to you I would be made whole. Look!"—and I held out the hands that at that moment were stilled of their trembling—"I am healed!"

The crowd began to murmur in amazement, many of them friends and neighbors who had loved me so long. But the voice of Jesus drowned out all other voices as he tenderly looked at me and said, "Daughter, thy faith hath made thee whole; go in peace."

My prayers were answered. I was well.

NO LONGER BLIND

*John 9:10-11; 24-25: "Therefore said they
unto him, How were thine eyes opened?
He answered and said, A man that is called
Jesus made clay, and anointed mine eyes,
and said unto me, Go to the pool of
Siloam, and wash; and I went and washed,
and I received sight.... Then again called
they the man that was blind, and said unto
him, Give God the praise; we know that
this man is a sinner. He answered and said,
Whether he be a sinner or no, I know not;
one thing I know, that, whereas I was
blind, now I see."*

Court proceedings in the synagogue on the
Sabbath were unheard of; yet here I was, being
questioned by the Pharisees. The silence of the
great hall was overwhelming as I stood there in
my humble garments. Bits of clay still clung to
my wet tunic, evidencing the eagerness with
which I had rushed to obey Jesus' command.
An insistent voice was demanding that I call

this man Jesus a sinner. The same questions were asked over and over again.

At last I could stand no more. Throwing my head back proudly and looking my accusers straight in the eye I answered in a voice loud enough to be heard through the open doors and into the courtyard.

"I have told you what happened! I don't know who or what this man Jesus is. I only know one thing: from the time I was born until this day I have never been able to see anything, but now," and I pounded the table in front of me for emphasis, "my eyes have been opened and I can see! Don't you understand? *I can see!*"

From outside there arose a great cheer as my words carried on the summer air, but the atmosphere within the room seemed to grow even darker. Ignoring the frowning countenances of the Pharisees who glared at me I continued.

"Well you know that I was blind from birth, for you asked my parents concerning this. They identified me as their son, and told you I had been born blind, but for fear of being cast from the synagogue they held their tongues about the manner in which I was made whole. 'Go and ask him,' they said. 'He is of age and must speak for himself.'

"You came to me and I told you the whole story. As Jesus passed by where I sat begging along the roadside his disciples asked, 'Master, who did sin, this man or his parents, that he was born blind?' Jesus told them we had not sinned, and that the glory of God's works would be shown in me. I could feel the silence that met his statement and then heard someone come and kneel before me.

"My eyes were covered with something cool, and my ears, which had long been tuned to hear the slightest sound, could hear the whisper among his followers: 'See! He has taken spittle and common dirt from the ground and has made clay!' Most of all I could feel the healing touch of the gentle fingers on my face. Then a deep voice spoke, 'Go, wash in the pool of Siloam.'

"A friend helped me along the path to the pool, a little way from the place where I begged. The day was warm so instead of merely kneeling by the water and washing my face I first walked into it to cool myself; then bending my face down, I washed away the clay from my sightless eyes.

"For a moment the great brightness that met my vision blurred all else. Than, as I became

42

accustomed to the light, I beheld the beauty of my surroundings. The clear water in which I stood, the sky with its fleecy white clouds—these I had seen only in my mind as they were described to me. Now for the first time I could actually see the beauty of the world around me.

"On the grassy bank stood my friends and neighbors who had followed to see what, if anything, would happen. They stood as if struck dumb as I went from one to another, recognizing them from descriptions I had been given and shouting, 'I can see—I can see!' They could hardly believe it was really their neighbor, the blind beggar, who stood among them, and it was decided I should come to the Pharisees for questioning. This is why I came."

* * *

The synagogue was filled with angry murmurs and the chief priest spoke. "You have been healed by a man who does not believe in God, for he breaks the Sabbath!"

Another priest turned and spoke, "But how can a sinner work miracles? Obviously this man was blind; now he sees. It is that simple, yet it is a miracle!"

Within seconds they were quarreling with

each other concerning my sight being restored, and how, and why.

Once again they turned to me, seeking to trick me into giving evidence against my healer. I could contain my anger no longer and shouted at them, "Since the world began, no one has ever opened the eyes of the blind save it be God! If this man were not of God he could do nothing!" And with a sudden rush I added, "It is your eyes that need to be opened even more than mine. My whole life was spent unable to see, yet you condemn the man who opened both my eyes and a new world to me, because he did it on the Sabbath!"

This was too much for them. "How dare you—you who were born in sin—to teach us?" they demanded, and I was cast out of the synagogue and forbidden to return. I suppose I should have been sad, but instead my heart was so full of rejoicing that I leaped and shouted all the way to my cottage.

In my excitement I had forgotten to eat. I took a few dates and some cheese and sat eating in my little garden watching the glorious sunset and the coming of twilight. Only one who has been blind and then suddenly sees could have appreciated the flaming rays and purple shadows that evening as I did. Their beauty was beyond description.

44

A few stars had come out when a soft step behind me told of someone's approach. Well I knew that step, even before Jesus came into view. At first I could not see his face clearly as he asked, "Do you believe on the Son of God?"

I thought for a moment before replying. "Who is he, Lord, that I might believe on him?"

Stepping a little closer Jesus said, "You have both seen him and it is he that talks with you."

The cloud that had covered the moon suddenly shifted and light streamed into the garden—the same brilliance I had seen when my eyes were first opened there in the little stream feeding the pool of Siloam. In the radiance the face of Jesus was clearly illumined, and I beheld the glory of that face.

Falling to my knees before him I proclaimed, "You are the light. Lord, I believe."

His piercing gaze held me transfixed for a moment. Then looking into his eyes I saw tears start, and at last I understood: This truly was the Son of God; he had come into the world that all who would might see. No longer need men be blind—no longer was I blind—for not only my eyes but my mind and heart had been opened. No more would I walk in darkness but in the radiant light of the Lord Jesus Christ, Son of the living God.

THE LAST HOST

Mark 14:10-15: "And the first day of un-
leavened bread, when they killed the passover,
his disciples said unto him, Where wilt thou
that we go and prepare, that thou mayest eat
the passover? And he sendeth forth two of his
disciples, and saith unto them, Go ye into the
city, and there shall meet you a man bearing a
pitcher of water; follow him. And whereso-
ever he shall go in, say ye to the good man of
the house, The Master saith, Where is the
guest chamber, where I shall eat the passover
with my disciples? And he will show you a
large upper room, furnished and prepared;
there make ready for us.

"And his disciples went forth and came into
the city, and found as he had said unto them;
and they made ready the passover. And in the
evening he cometh with the twelve."

The years behind me are many, yet I can still
picture those strange happenings as if they had
occurred only yesterday. It was the first day of the

feast of unleavened bread. My household was busy with all the preparations for the Passover meal that would be eaten that evening. The large upper room of our home was being carefully cleaned and set up, for all of us looked forward to this time of remembrance. The cooks in the kitchen were preparing the required food and my most faithful servant had gone to the well for a pitcher of fresh water. He returned with a strange look in his eyes. Two men had followed him home, and they wished to speak with me, the master of the house.

As I awaited their coming, I was amazed to find myself trembling; for what reason I knew not. They entered quietly and the taller of the two spoke: "Good man of the house, the Master saith, 'Where is the guest chamber, where I shall eat the passover with my disciples?' "

I stared at them for a moment, then, to my own amazement, found myself showing them the large upper room which we had furnished and prepared that morning. As I watched them making ready for the feast I inquired, "Who is your Master?" and swift and proud was their reply: "Jesus of Nazareth."

In joy I hastened to tell my wife the wonderful news. Was this not the same Jesus who had healed the crippled boy next door? . . . And our home had been chosen for this honor! It was almost more than I could do to keep from running into the street and shouting the glad news.

The hours sped quickly by, and as the shadows of evening were lengthening into darkness, Jesus and the twelve gathered there in our upper room. The night was clear, and much of what took place was audible to me as my wife and I sat below, barely comprehending this honor.

As they sat eating, Jesus spoke to his disciples in a voice filled with greater sadness than I had ever heard and told them that one of the little group would betray him. His disciples asked sorrowfully, "Could it be I? Is it I?"

He answered, "It is one of the twelve who dippeth with me in the dish. Woe to that man by whom the Son of Man is betrayed! Good were it for that man if he had never been born."

A chill seemed to descend on my heart. Could one of Jesus' closest companions betray him? It hardly seemed possible, and yet could he be mistaken? I wanted to cry out, but again he was speaking. He was blessing the bread and breaking it, then giving it to his disciples.

"Take it and eat. . . . Do this in remembrance of my body . . . for as oft as ye do this, ye will remember this hour that I was with you."

Again he paused, then taking the cup of wine he blessed it and gave it to his disciples and said to them, "This is in remembrance of my blood which is shed for many, and the new testament which I give unto you . . . and as oft as ye do this, ye will remember me in this hour that I was with you and drank with you of this cup, even the last time in my ministry."

The time had passed so rapidly it was difficult to believe that the Passover feast was over. One of the disciples, a dazed look on his face, left first—rushing down the stairs and away into the night. I could hear the soft strains of a hymn being sung, and soon Jesus and his other disciples had gone from our home.

I couldn't forget the look in his eyes as he thanked me for the hospitality of our home . . . and then he was gone. I threw on a cloak and hurried after him, but he and his disciples were far ahead. The night was cold, so at last I started toward home. . . . had I known what was to befall him, I would never have turned back that strange and wonderful night when I was Jesus' last host.

THE AWAKENING

Luke 23:48: "Now when the centurion saw what was done, he glorified God, saying, Certainly this was a righteous man."

"In all my years with the Roman army I have never seen happenings such as I witnessed today. Those crucifixions have always bothered me. I hate them, yet they are part of my job. It is my duty to conduct them. I have my orders and ask no questions. But today was different, for today I commanded the soldiers who crucified the Son of God!"

My wife's hands that had been quietly folded on her lap were trembling now. Her expression was one of fear, disbelief, and utter amazement. "What do you mean?" she whispered. "I have never heard you speak so."

"I have never felt so," I dully replied. "There was nothing I could do. . . . By the time I realized the truth about him, he was dead."

She could make no reply and for a long time only the sound of the small fire crackling in the grate could be heard. At last she spoke. "Perhaps it would help if you could tell me what it was like. Since I cannot walk and no one has come today I really do not know what happened. That strange and horrible darkness for three hours—what did it mean? Can you speak of these things to me?"

In the silence that followed I could feel my heart pounding the way it had pounded there on the hill. In the distance a voice began to speak. I recognized the hoarse tones as my own.

"There was something different about this one from the very first, I felt it when we were called in. He never once pleaded for mercy or begged for his life when the sentence was pronounced. Throughout the whole trial, if you can call it such, he seemed to sense what was coming—and in a way he seemed almost relieved to get on with it. He was hurt, bruised, and weak. While carrying the cross he stumbled and fell until we pulled a man from the crowd to help him carry it.

"At the top of the hill we all noticed the contrast between this one and the other two. The air was filled with their groans and curses, yet he made no struggle nor did he cry out, Once in a low voice he said, 'Father, forgive them; for they know not what they do.'

"I didn't like it—I didn't like it at all. I tell you,

the feeling on that hill was uncanny. It wasn't the little group of mourners. It wasn't even that his mother was there—there are always groups of mourners and sometimes family members present. No, it was something more—something in the very air itself that you could almost reach out and touch.

"As usual, my men cast lots for the garments, but somehow over it all lay that unexplainable difference. Perhaps it was the sign over the center cross, 'King of the Jews.' Never before, even in derision, had such a sign been permitted. The people and rulers mocked him, as did my soldiers, saying, 'If thou be King of the Jews, save thyself,' but he did not answer them.

"One of the two thieves also mocked him, telling him to save them, but the other one rebuked him. 'Are you not afraid of God?' he asked. 'We are being punished for our deeds, and rightly so, but this man is innocent of any wrongdoing.' Strange words for him to say—and Pilate too had spoken them. The second thief said to Jesus, 'Lord, remember me when thou comest into thy kingdom.' Jesus answered, and a look of love seemed to touch the furrowed brow: 'Verily I say unto thee; today shalt thou be with me in Paradise.'

"I noticed that darkness had fallen over the city. Great clouds of inky blackness were surrounding the hill, yet it was only the sixth hour. I looked at my men; no longer were they jesting but, like me, were tensely waiting for it to be over. Three hours we stayed in that place of gloom, and at the ninth hour Jesus cried with a loud voice, 'Father, into thy hands I commend my spirit.' At long last it was finished.

"There was a crack as though the heavens themselves had split open, and the blackness was intense, but just before that awful moment I had looked up into his face and then I knew—he was indeed the Son of God. I cried out something to that effect and as the rain and tears poured down my face I reached out to him—but it was too late.

"I left Marcus in charge and found my way home then. People in the streets were trying to move the rubble caused by the terrible earthquake. I heard someone say the graves had opened and they had seen the people walking the streets. As I passed the great temple, the veil was split from top to bottom.

"But what are these things to me? I only know one thing—I crucified the Son of God! How can I live with that knowledge? If I had only recognized him sooner I could have asked his forgiveness, and

53

you know, I really think he would have forgiven me. But it is too late now! What shall I do? Better were it that I had died there on that hill of Calvary with the two thieves than to suffer the rest of my life, haunted by his shadow.''

* * *

The faraway voice I recognized as my own ceased. I became aware I had unknowingly crossed the room to kneel at my wife's crippled feet. She gently placed her hands upon my shoulders. Although her face was wet with tears, in her eyes was a radiance I could not understand.

"Don't you see?" she said. "He understood—and he forgave you—even before you knew there was anything to ask forgiveness for! When he said, 'Father, forgive them; for they know not what they do,' he was not only referring to the crowd of priests and onlookers but to you, and your men. You had not plotted against him; you had not shouted 'crucify' in the streets; you had not cried out for the release of Bar-Abbas. You had only followed orders. It was you he prayed for, that you might be forgiven!"

I gazed into her eyes, but again I was seeing the eyes of the King of the Jews, Jesus. His look and words were ringing in my brain and suddenly I knew my wife was right—I was forgiven! Striding to the door I clasped my cloak around me.

As she leaned forward to ask, "Where are you going?" the shawl slipped from her useless legs, but she seemed not to notice.

I paused in the doorway to answer, and my words expressed the hope of the world to both her ears and mine. "I remember now. . . . After they took Jesus from the courtroom one of my men was there. He heard the priests ask Pilate to put a guard at the tomb, for there was a popular belief that Jesus would rise again from the dead on the third day. . . ." I hesitated, then continued, "I believe I will volunteer for that watch."

The countenance of my wife seemed to glow with an unearthly light as she slowly nodded her head then rose to her feet, straight and strong, and proudly walked to my side.

UNAWARE

Luke 24:12, 13: "And behold, two of them went that same day to a village called Emmaus, which was from Jerusalem about threescore furlongs. And they talked together of all these things which had happened."

"It is finished!" The cry rang through the darkness that had fallen so strangely over the hillside. Suddenly a mighty crack of thunder sounded and the earth on which I stood was shaken—shaken even as my faith had been in the past few days. I stood on the hillside looking at the one I had believed was the Messiah. The rain beat down upon me, the earth rocked, and the heavens rang with the echoes of his words: "Finished—finished—finished."

At last I could stand no more. I turned away and the despair in my heart was as dark as the day had become. Although my back was now to the three crosses, they seemed to be etched on my mind. Somehow I stumbled to the house of my kinsman Cleopas where the Passover had been spent. He too was shaken, almost in a stupor. No words were exchanged; there was nothing left to say.

The next few days will always be a blurred memory in the corridors of my mind. I had been stricken by the crucifixion of Jesus so that nothing seemed to matter at all. Late in the afternoon of the first day of the week we began to hear strange stories. It was said that the Magdalene woman, Mary, had visited the tomb—only to find it empty! And that Jesus had appeared to her, alive and beautiful. It was hard to understand. . . . How could it be?

Knowing I was still rather stunned, Cleopas insisted on accompanying me when I felt I must go home to Emmaus that day. He wanted me to stay with him just a little longer, but I felt I should get back to my family. They would be anxiously awaiting me; news of the past weekend's events traveled fast, and they would be wondering about me.

As we started down the dusty road to Emmaus, I suddenly found myself pouring out my feelings to Cleopas in a way I had never done before. I told him how I had prayed, watched, and waited since I was a child for the time when the Messiah would come. I had seen many who proclaimed themselves such, who rose in popularity then were destroyed.

But this time it had been different. This man Jesus had changed lives. He touched a withered arm and it was healed; he smiled into troubled hearts and they became well. I had followed him, as had Cleopas, and I had grown to love him. I seemed filled with a burning Spirit when he was near. Along with the others I had joyfully anticipated his reign as King of the earth . . . and now he was dead!

Cleopas trudged silently by my side a few paces then said, "But what of Mary's story? She was always so close to Jesus, because he had forgiven her so much. How do you feel about her experience this morning?"

I paused and reflected on his question. It was true. Mary had faithfully served him from the very moment his Spirit had first touched her life.

Before I could answer a stranger approached us. I hadn't noticed others on the road, but then Cleopas and I had been so absorbed in our conversation that we had paid little attention to anything else.

In a pleasant voice the stranger asked if he might walk with us. As we nodded assent he inquired, "What are you speaking of that makes you so sad?"

Cleopas and I found ourselves impolitely staring

at the stranger. Where could he have been not to have heard of the happenings in Jerusalem? To cover our amazement we began telling him of all that had transpired. We even told how Mary and the disciples had found the tomb empty earlier that day.

When the stranger again spoke he said to us, "O fools and slow of heart to believe all that the prophets have spoken. Ought not Christ to have suffered these things and to enter into his glory?" Then he went on to quote Moses and all the prophets whose scripture told of the Christ to come.

Never had the seven and a half miles from Jerusalem seemed so short. As he spoke my heart burned within me, and looking at Cleopas I saw that he was experiencing the same sensations. When we reached the outskirts of the village, the lights of evening were already twinkling. Our new friend (for we could no longer call him a stranger) started on over the hills to the next village, but we insisted that he stay with us, for darkness was fast approaching. My wife had the evening meal prepared and soon we were sitting down together. Something in our new friend's manner caused me to turn to him saying, "Sir, will you not bless the bread?"

59

A look of radiance crossed his face as he lifted his hands, blessed and broke the bread, and handed it to us. For a moment I felt paralyzed, then every part of my body trembled. "You are the Christ!" I whispered in awe, for at last my earth-blinded eyes could see. . . . They had been opened by the sight of the jagged scars in the palms of his hands as he blessed the bread.

Once more that look of radiance crossed his face. Once more those torn hands were lifted as in blessing. Then he was gone.

"Wait!" I cried, as we rushed to the door. But all I could hear was an echo, "Peace," and the road ahead lay empty. He had gone.

Cleopas was the first to speak. "We should have known! Did not our hearts burn within us when he told us the scriptures?"

"Hurry," I commanded. "He cannot have gone far. We will go back to Jerusalem; we will overtake him on the way." In a matter of moments we had wrapped our cloaks around us against the night air and were on the road.

The miles fell away from our feet as we hurried to Jerusalem, but we overtook no weary traveler. Ahead we could see the walls of the city and we knew he had gone elsewhere, but still we kept our steady pace forward. . . . Had we not seen the living Christ? We must hasten to tell the good news.

When we reached the home Jesus had so often stayed in we found the eleven disciples and a few other followers gathered together in the upper room. One was saying, "The Lord is risen indeed; he has appeared to Simon." Cleopas and I looked at one another. "He *has* risen," I cried out in joy. We told of the walk to Emmaus and how we had not recognized him because our hearts and eyes were blinded with our own grief.

Without warning, he was in our midst. There had been no knock at the door. He appeared the same way he had disappeared earlier that evening. The disciples were frightened and we fell to our knees. "Peace be with you," he said, and it was the same beloved voice that had blessed the bread in our home.

He showed us his hands and feet. While we were filled with joy, our minds seemed unable to grasp the very evidence before us until he took fish and honeycomb and ate. At last we rejoiced! How strange it was that it was so difficult for us to believe what we wanted so much to believe. He had to prove to us that he was more than spirit—that he had a human appetite—before we could finally accept the fact that he was alive again.

The evening that followed was one I will never forget, for the ministry he gave was to carry me through all the heartbreak and persecution that followed. The road he had called us to walk as witnesses proved to be long and hard, but never once did I turn back from the memory of One who once walked with me along another road—the dusty seven and a half miles to Emmaus.

HE SAW GOD

*Book of Mormon, Ether 1:8-11, 38-41, 94:
"And the Brother of Jared being a large
and a mighty man, and being a man highly
favored of the Lord, for Jared his brother said
unto him, Cry unto the Lord, that he will not
confound us that we may not understand our
words. And it came to pass that the Brother
of Jared did cry unto the Lord, and the Lord
had compassion upon Jared; therefore he did
not confound the language of Jared; and
Jared and his brother were not confounded. . . . And the Lord had compassion
upon their friends, and their families also,
that they were not confounded.*

*"And it came to pass at the end of four
years, that the Lord came again unto the
Brother of Jared, and stood in a cloud and
talked with him. And for the space of three
hours did the Lord talk with the Brother of
Jared, and chastened him because he remembered not to call upon the name of the Lord.
And the Brother of Jared repented of the evil
which he had done. . . . And the Lord said*

unto him, I will forgive thee and thy brethren of their sins; but thou shalt not sin any more. . . .

"And the Lord commanded the Brother of Jared to go down out of the mount from the presence of the Lord, and write the things which he had seen; and they were forbidden to come unto the children of men, until after that he should be lifted up upon the cross."

I have been commanded by the Lord to write and seal up those things he has shown me—yet I hardly know where to begin! As I ponder the scenes I have been shown, the magnificent past and the future still to be unrolled, I find it difficult even now to fully comprehend it all. There is within me a burning that must be satisfied, the need to know that you who hear my words in the days to come will understand how it was with me. Hearken, O ye people; listen to my story and heed my words, for the Almighty One wishes to reveal himself to you, as he did to me, the brother of Jared.

But wait! I must look back that you might understand those events leading up to this moment.

I am a large man, tall, full-bodied, and strong. The Lord has favored me with health and happiness, but most of all, with his Spirit. At the time of the great tower, when all around our entire world seemed to be changing, my brother came to me, asking me to cry to the Lord. The language of the people was being confounded and he could not bear it that we might be separated from our families and friends—yes, even from each other—by the strange barrier God had sent to earth.

I talked with God and he had compassion upon us; not only was our language spared but he led us out of the land and to the edge of the great sea. Oh, how happy we were that God had spared us! My heart was filled with thankfulness, and as we reached the sea which we named Moriancumer I sang praises to the Lord for his mercy.

Looking back, it is hard to understand how I could so quickly forget the wonderful blessings we had been given. We pitched our tents and each day seemed busier than the one before. We prospered there on the banks of the great sea, and as time went by I failed to call upon the Lord. Everything seemed to be going so well it did not seem as important to talk with him as it had been in our days of great need. After all, he had guided us here by his own hand. I realize now this was the work of the evil one to lull us into a false feeling that all was well.

Four years passed and still we dwelt by the sea. One morning I awakened very early—it was the hour between dawn and sunrise—and I felt that I should go forth. No one stirred as I left the encampment; not even a dog barked. I climbed a high hill just as the rays of the sun were beginning to reflect on the sea.

In the distance a cloud appeared, growing in size until it covered the hill on which I stood. I fell to my knees and a voice spoke from the cloud, a voice I well knew but had not sought for so long.

For three hours the Lord talked with me, and he chastened me because I had not remembered to call on him. In deepest repentance I cried out, "O Lord, forgive me! I am a sinful man and I need your presence to guide me. Forgive my brethren, for I have not called upon thee, and have caused them to sin against thee!" And from the cloud the voice of God again spoke, bringing forgiveness, but telling me to sin no more, for his Spirit would not always strive with man.

The Lord went on to tell me about the choice land to which he would lead us. Throughout the days that followed, he guided us in making barges and preparing for a great sea journey.

At last the barges were finished, but they had no light, so I sought out the Lord. Taking sixteen small white stones, I asked him to touch the stones with his finger that they might shine in the vessels to provide light on the long journey.

Suddenly I fell to the ground in fear. My eyes had been opened, for as the finger of God touched the stones, I saw that finger and it had the appearance of flesh and blood, as the finger of a man. I cried out, "O Lord, I did not know you had flesh and blood!" Then the Lord spoke, telling me he would take upon him flesh and blood, and that never before had one come to him with such great faith. And then he spoke again, asking if I would believe the words which he would speak.

"Yes, Lord," I replied. "I know that you speak the truth, for you are a God of truth and cannot lie."

The next moment a blinding light filled the air around me, and looking up I beheld the Lord Jesus Christ, who was prepared from the beginning of the world to redeem his people. I saw that I was indeed created after his own image and that all men were created after his image. The sky and sea and even the earth upon which I stood seemed to recede, and in their place came a procession of scenes—scenes of all the inhabitants of the earth who had ever lived. The scenes continued to appear, now changing to show all that would come until the end of time. I saw the last walk of Jesus to the cross on Calvary, and the resurrection. I saw the period of darkness that followed, and at last I saw the coming forth of these words, and how they would be understood through the two stones I had also been commanded to seal up.

* * *

My writings are nearly ended, yet once again I am seeing you—you who are hundreds of years in the future. Some of you will read my story and will not heed it. Some of you may scorn or condemn me for the times I failed to call on God. Some of you will have faith, and will relive my experiences.

But to all of you I say, These words are true, for I write them exactly as I saw them and as they were shown to me by the Lord Jesus Christ, and they will be hidden away that you might believe.

THE WITNESS

Tonight I went again to the thicket surrounding the pool of water called Mormon. I knew it was dangerous for me to be seen there, yet I yearned to find meaning in life. Only in so doing would I be able to blot out the memory of the past months and be free.

The sequence of events leading to the present started slowly. The first stirrings within me came when the man Abinadi rose up over two years ago and began preaching repentance to us who were living under the rule of King Noah. He told us if we did not repent the Lord God would deliver us into the hands of our enemy. King Noah was enraged and ordered this man taken. I was one who went for Abinadi, but somehow he had been spirited away and we were unable to find him.

During the following two years King Noah and his court continued to live in wickedness. I must confess I found it exciting to be welcomed on occasion to his banquets and feasts; still a part of me seemed to stand back aghast at the things I did. I would lift my wine glass high and try to drown out all else, but never did I quite overcome that involuntary feeling of distaste with myself in those moments.

One day a stranger appeared in the crowds and lifting his voice he prophesied the doom that would befall King Noah and the people if they would not repent. Knowing how this had angered the king before, we bound the man and took him to the halls of the palace for questioning. As I guarded the entrance of the great room I was amazed. The priests sought to trap him, but in every instance his answers made the priests and their questions seem foolish. His face shone with an almost frightening brilliance, and a chord in my heart throbbed with the truth of his words.

"Touch me not," he warned as we were commanded by the king to seize the prophet. "God will smite you if you lay your hands upon me, for I have not delivered the message which the Lord sent me to deliver."

Seeing the luster of his face we fell back. My heart beat faster. This was no ordinary stranger standing before us. Surely this was Abinadi who had returned disguised and who even now continued speaking with power and authority. "You have taught iniquity," he proclaimed. "You have not taught the commandments of Moses handed down to you from your fathers. Woe unto you!"

He paused then went on to tell of one who would come, even Christ, the Son of God, and how he would be rejected and crucified. He spoke of the resurrection, and of eternal life, then said, "Had you not ought to tremble and repent of your sins, and remember that only in and through Christ ye can be saved? If you teach the Law of Moses, also teach that it is a shadow of those things which are to come; teach that redemption cometh through Christ the Lord, who is the very eternal Father. Amen."

For a moment there was stunned silence. Then the hush of the room was shattered by King Noah's shriek, "This man must be put to death!" The king's crowd of malingerers took up the cry, "Death to the prophet who dares to speak so to the king!"

In the melee a single voice, filled with urgency, rang out. "Stop!" Instantly the noise ceased. In astonishment we turned to see who spoke. My heart sang as I saw my young friend Alma, the descendant of Nephi, making his way to the king. "Do not be angry with Abinadi," he pleaded, and his face seemed to reflect the glory of the prophet's countenance. "Let him go in peace."

It seemed impossible for the king to grow angrier, yet his face turned almost black with rage as he ordered Alma from the room. The door had no sooner closed behind Alma than the king called out again, "Go after him and slay him!"

This was the opportunity for which I'd hoped. "Go that way," I shouted to the others. "I'll take this street; he cannot have gone far." Running with desperate speed I burst into his dwelling place. "Go, Alma, they are coming," I whispered. He paused only long enough to clasp my hand warmly and was gone.

"We are too late," I told the king's servants who came. "He has fled." An overturned chair confirmed his hasty departure and we hurried back to the palace.

By the time we arrived back at the great hall, Abinadi had been bound and cast into prison, and King Noah and his wicked priests were already deep in conference.

Three days passed, intense days of waiting, while over the city hung a pall. The atmosphere itself seemed to cry out in protest. At last King Noah summoned Abinadi.

"You have said God himself will come down among the children of men, and for this cause you are worthy of death. But if you will recall all the words of evil about me and my people, you will be released."

The priests smugly waited with folded arms for Abinadi to deny his words. He carefully looked at each one. Then he spoke and his voice was a whip that cracked the hard shell of hypocrisy surrounding them.

"I will not recall my words, for they are true. If you slay me it is innocent blood you shed and this will testify against you at the last day."

The face of King Noah paled, and with shaking hands he leaned forward as if he would order Abinadi released; but the priests began to call out, "He has reviled the King!" A rush of red rose to the king's face. For a moment he struggled between fear of God's judgments and pride in himself. Fury overcame his hesitance and his next command was shouted: "He is to be burned at the stake."

The following scene was one of horror as the priests took Abinadi to kill him for speaking the truth. The flames surrounded him, providing a background that was etched indelibly on the minds of the onlookers. From the midst of the fire he cried out that afflictions would fall on the people. I can still hear his last words, "O God, receive my soul!" With a glorious smile he raised his hands to heaven, sealing the truth of his words with his death.

I turned away, shriveled and scorched inside, even as Abinadi had been. A strange fever seemed to possess me in the days following; I was burning hot and there was no release until in the midst of it all a Presence came to me.

"Who are you?" I whispered, yet knowing it could be none other than Abinadi's Christ who now placed cooling hands on me. At last I regained consciousness, and while I could no longer see him, yet the Presence lingered with me.

When my strength returned I sought out Alma, who I had heard was secretly preaching the words of Abinadi—he had recorded them all while in hiding. At first only a small group came, then more and more people made their way to the waters of Mormon for baptism.

All these things were passing through my mind while I walked the wooded trail to the place of gathering. When I arrived Alma was speaking. He beckoned and I went forward, only to pause dumbfounded at his words.

"This is the friend of whom I told you," he said slowly, then placed his arms around my shoulders. "You were a witness to all that happened. Will you not tell us about it?"

The world spun around me. I looked into the sea of eager, upturned faces. What could I say? How could I excuse the passive part I had played, even after recognition of Abinadi as a man of God had come to me? Once again I felt the Presence even closer to me than before. "Tell them of Abinadi, . . . and of me."

Slowly I began my story, and as I spoke, it was possible for me to relive the painful experiences and to be completely honest with these people. At last I ceased; the only sound disturbing the silence was the soft weeping of some of the women. In the stillness, once more my voice broke forth. "Yes, I witnessed it all—God forgive me! I never defended Abinadi. . . . I wish I too had died with him in the flames; perhaps then I might have found peace!"

Alma raised his hand. "No, my friend, the time for you is not yet. Abinadi's desire was to be a witness. It was all he ever hoped for, all he dreamed of." He paused, then continued: "You are the one who can continue his ministry. You must not let his dream die, for through you, as a witness, Abinadi lives and tells his story over and over again. This is your calling."

My heart beat faster with sudden hope. Like a man grasping at straws I clutched his hand. "You mean I could be forgiven?"

Alma smiled. "All who repent and become humble can be baptized in his name and be forgiven," and he motioned to the waters of Mormon. Without a word I rose and entered the stream with him.

"May the Spirit of the Lord be poured out upon you," he said, and the feeling between us as he clasped my hands was a bond that could never be broken.

Once again I beheld the Presence visibly. It was Abinadi's Christ, yet now he was also my Christ. I had been obedient to his commands and the smile he wore showed me he was pleased. The words of Alma continued to ring in my heart as the Christ and I started the first steps of our journey together. Only He knew where it would lead— perhaps even to the same fiery death Abinadi had experienced—but I knew it really did not matter. As long as I live, that Presence will guide the footsteps of the man I have become—his witness.

ENCOUNTER

Mosiah 11:159: "Now the sons of Mosiah were numbered among the unbelievers; and also one of the sons of Alma was numbered among them, he being called Alma, after his father; nevertheless he became a very wicked and an idolatrous man."

I looked into the face of my son as he lay stricken before us. It seemed impossible that the merry, golden-haired child he had once been could have become the man lying there. His face was hard, for the rough life he led was leaving its mark. "Oh, Alma, my son," my heart cried out, "how have we failed you? Why did you leave your childhood faith and seek out wickedness?"

My husband, the older Alma, and I had known part of the story now told us by the sons of Mosiah, for although the work they had been doing was kept secret, news had begun to trickle back of the wickedness they were stirring up. It almost broke our hearts to know that this son was attempting to destroy the church of God. He had

77

created dissension and arguing, and in so doing had enabled the enemy of God to gain control over people's hearts.

Now he lay before us as one dead; weak, helpless, and dumb he had been carried to his father by the sons of Mosiah following their experience on the road outside the city walls.

My attention snapped back to Himni, who was telling what had happened. He too seemed dazed and was speaking slowly. "We were riding along that grassy field just outside the city. Our hearts were rejoicing, for we had been able to influence many in the past weeks. We had found that those who could not be shaken by arguments were subject to flattery and we played upon their pride until they too followed us.

"It was just at the little knoll overlooking the stream that a cloud appeared. The sky was clear, so we dismounted to investigate. With a snort our horses broke and ran. We were angry and started to chase them, but the cloud surrounded us, and a figure descended from it. In fear we fell to the ground, huddling there as a voice like thunder shook the earth. We did not understand, but he cried out again and we perceived it was an angel of the Lord.

"He told Alma to arise and asked why he

78

persecuted God's church. The angel explained that nothing could destroy it except the transgression of the people. Trembling, we listened to his words. Alma's father's prayers had been heard, and it was because of his faith that the angel had come to show us God's power and authority. He told Alma to heed those words and seek no more to destroy God's work. Again we fell to the earth and the shining figure was gone as suddenly as he had come. We knew that only God's power could have shaken the earth and our very souls. Even though the words had been addressed to Alma, my brothers and I knew they were a judgment on all who sought to hinder God's work in even the slightest manner."

Himni's voice ceased, and looking into his face I saw a new humility, a gentleness, that had started to grow. In amazement I turned to his brothers, standing there before me; the same look was upon their faces.

Himni spoke again, sadly. "When we recovered our senses Alma could not speak or stand—no, he could not even move his hands—so we came here."

In the quiet that followed we all gazed upon Alma, helpless from God's chastening. My husband began to rejoice, for he knew his prayers had been heard by God and even now were being answered by the power of God. He sent for the church leaders and caused a great multitude to assemble to behold God's power. He met with the priests. For two days and nights they fasted and prayed that God would open Alma's mouth and restore strength to his limbs, and also that the eyes and hearts of the people would be opened.

During those two nights I spent much time by the bedside of my son. He was fully conscious, for his eyes seemed to plead with me. Into them had crept some of the expression now worn by the sons of Mosiah, who even now were going about testifying to the people of their encounter with God.

Just before dawn that ended the second night, I sat looking down as I held my son's hand. I knew God's judgment was upon him, and that it was righteous, yet it was hard for me to accept his paralysis. He was more helpless than he had been as a baby. He could do nothing for himself. It was like being born all over again. My mind quickened at the thought. Born again . . . of course! He had chosen to lead his life in opposition to God's laws. Now for God to use him, he must become completely dependent upon God for all of life, that he might begin to grow straight, strong, and true.

There was a slight pressure on my hand, and then I saw Alma smiling at me. My cry of joy brought my husband to the bedside in time to witness Alma getting out of bed. "Let me speak to the people," he whispered. As he spoke his voice grew stronger and strength flowed into his limbs.

Making his way to the open courtyard he called, "Be of good comfort. I have repented of my sins and am redeemed of the Lord. . . . Behold, I am born of the Spirit!"

The people listened in awe as he told them of God's words, that all must be born again or they could never be in the kingdom of God. He confessed his wickedness and told how a merciful and loving God had snatched him from his torment. The sons of Mosiah were near him as he spoke, and the early morning light flooded the courtyard where they stood.

The same light flooded my soul as my husband and I stood with hands clasped, hearts beating together. Truly our prayers had been answered, for Alma and the sons of Mosiah had encountered God in a way few people ever do. At the same time we understood that every living soul who seeks with all his or her heart will encounter God in a meaningful way—perhaps not in the voice of an angel, perhaps not in a vision, but in a way needed most at that time.

Thanksgiving filled us. Our son who had been lost was found. As the morning light brightened to light up every countenance, we knew it ushered in a new day.

HE GAVE HIS SINS AWAY

Alma 12 and 13

My heart is troubled. My sleep is broken with strange dreams. I have never felt this way before and I feel drawn in many directions. A decision is necessary, yet how can I know which way I should go?

A few days ago my husband Lamoni, who is king over all the land, returned from a journey greatly shaken. He had met our son Lamoni with a Nephite, one called Ammon. They had been on their way to Middoni to arrange for the release of some other Nephites who had been captured and were in prison.

My husband shared his experience with me. "The anger that rushed over me was blinding," he confessed. "I commanded that our son slay this man who would deceive us as the Nephites deceived our fathers, and that he return immediately to Ishmael. He flatly refused to do either. I raised my hand to smite this disobedient son but the stranger commanded me to stop. I attacked him but he repelled my blows and gained

83

a superior position. He could have killed me but instead he made demands that I not smite Lamoni, but allow him to live and rule his part of the kingdom as he felt right; that I release the Nephites from prison; and that I not be angry with my son or he, Ammon, would still slay me."

After a moment's shocked silence he went on. "When I saw the love he had for our son and that he really had no desire to slay me, I was astonished. I agreed to his terms that my life might be spared. But I also invited Ammon and his brothers to come here, for his words touched me greatly, and I am desirous of learning more."

I had listened to my husband's words in stunned silence. "You mean you would have slain Lamoni?" I whispered.

He paced up and down, saying, "Yes! The power of evil was so strong within me that I would have killed our son if Ammon had not stopped me." I could hardly believe my ears. There had always been great love one for another in our family. To think it could come to this!

A servant tapped gently at the open door. "My Lord, there are strangers here to see you, Nephites. One says he is called Aaron and has been led by someone called God to see you, that you know his brother Ammon."

"Show them in," my husband commanded. Suddenly I rose to my feet. "I cannot stay and hear these men! I will go to my room while you interview them."

A sense of foreboding filled me and several hours later I was not even surprised when one of the servants ran to me. "Come quickly!" she cried. "The master has fallen."

When I entered the hall my husband lay as if dead and the strangers stood above him. Had they killed him? I could find no sign of life.

"Take them and slay them!" I commanded the servants. "They have killed the king."

"We cannot do that, my lady," said old Thomas softly. Seeing my astonishment at his reply, he told me what had happened after I left the room.

"These men told the king wonderful things about the Great Spirit, whom they call God. The king asked how he might receive the great joy and eternal life they showed him, even unto forsaking his whole kingdom. The one called Aaron told him, 'You must bow down in faith, calling upon God, and believing you will receive—that is all.' When he had spoken the king knelt and called out that if there was a God to make himself known. He promised to give away all his sins to possess eternal life. When he finished speaking he fell to the earth and we ran for you. We dare not lay hands on these men for fear of what might happen to us."

My heart burned within me at his words and great was my fear that evil would fall on me. Nevertheless, I shouted for the servants to call the people to come slay these men who had cast some kind of spell, first upon my son and now upon my husband.

The tallest of the strangers, Aaron, raised his hand. "Wait." Lifting the king from the earth he said, "Stand," and strength returned to my husband.

With a cry of joy I ran to him. His face was aglow as he commanded our entire household to assemble. He ministered in such a way that truth was shown to each of us, and we too accepted the teachings Aaron and his brother brought to us. I rejoice in their words, and I rejoice in my husband, who laid aside royalty for humility when he gave his sins away.

ONE OF MY SONS

Alma 26

He stood there before me, a small, freckle-faced lad. His feet were sturdily set apart and an unruly lock of hair had escaped his helmet to dangle over one eye. "I want to be one of your sons, sir," he said simply.

Amazed at his request I stared curiously at his tattered garments. Scratched and torn, his hands were clasped firmly together. I began to feel admiration for this plucky youngster, and irritation at his presence subsided. Calling forth my sternest voice I spoke, "You should not be here. When you followed the two thousand young men who came to fight you would have starved if one of the guards had not discovered your plight and fed you. Why did you come?"

Even the smallest boy can wear dignity at times, and this lad stiffened even more. "I would have needed no help if my provisions had not been stolen. I wrapped enough in a sack to keep me on the journey, but while I slept a dog took it all." He paused, then continuing to look at me straight in the eye said, "My mother raised my brother and me; my father is dead. Just before she died she told me to take care of my brother. Even though he is older she knew I could help him. When everyone was preparing to come and he signed up I knew I too must become a son of Helaman." For the first time a look of fear crossed his face as he added, "You won't send me away?"

I scratched my head, wondering what to do. I had no spare man to take him back.

"Please let me speak again, sir," he pleaded. Nodding, I listened. "We have never fought," he said. "I overheard our captain telling you this. We are not afraid to die, for our mothers taught us that we must be free. My mother also said that if we only had faith in God and did not doubt, he would protect us. We all believe this is true."

A warm rush of feeling threatened to choke me. "So be it!" I snapped. "You will be in charge of my horse. See that he is well taken care of at all times!"

"Yes, *sir!*" he shouted and joy filled his eyes even though his soldierly stance never wavered.

"Dismissed!" I said, then, "Wait—what are you called?"

"I wish to be called Helaman, after you," he stated with a grin, then was gone.

With a chuckle at his impudence I turned back to my work. In the days that followed he held true. I never did find out his real name. The men called him by various names, but he conveniently did not seem to hear unless addressed as Helaman.

When all was in readiness we started our march. Never had my horse been so well groomed or my equipment so well cared for. The lad spent hours on his duties, never seeming to tire. I observed his brother, a fine young man as were all of my two thousand. My heart beat fast with pride in my "sons." I dreaded the day when some of them would be lost in battle.

We surrounded the Lamanites and as we fell upon them I bade the boy to keep back. His face gleamed. The fray was soon over, for the Lamanites delivered themselves and their weapons to us in short order. With heavy heart I took the lad with me that we might count the dead among my sons.

"There are none," he said.

I started in surprise. "Of course there are," I protested. "We cannot have come through such fighting with no casualties."

"There are none," he repeated with a smile, "God protects us. . . . See? . . ."

We made our way through the ranks, finding the injured but no dead. *Not one young man had lost his life in the battle for freedom.*

In the ensuing encounters with the Lamanites it was always the same. The fighting was fierce, yet I did not lose my sons.

After the last battle in which the Lamanites fled to the land of Nephi, I could not find "little Helaman" as the men now called him. No one seemed to have seen him. We searched and searched, but he was nowhere to be found. By now the entire camp was alarmed. Had he been carried away by the Lamanites? At last in desperation I went to the stable to get my horse. I would try to trace the youngster we had all grown to love so much.

When I reached the stable I heard muffled sobs. There he lay, beside my horse. His arm was crudely bandaged and bloodstains showed through. Raising his head he said brokenly, "I'm sorry, sir. One of the arrows—it was aimed for me. Your horse jumped just then and the arrow only grazed me, but," with a fresh burst of sobbing, "it got him. I didn't take good care of him like you said. I have failed you."

Gently I lifted him to his feet. "You are truly a son of mine," I told him. "Sometimes God requires sacrifices. Many of my men are wounded, yet all live, and we are free."

He raised his head, and through the tears shone understanding. "Thank you, my father," he said, and in that moment the youngest of my sons became a man.

HEAR YE HIM

Helaman 5 (paraphrased): "I give you a sign: five years from now shall the Son of God come to redeem all people who believe on his name, and for two days and a night no darkness will come. A new star will appear in the heavens such as has never before been seen.... And I give you a sign of his death; for three days there shall be no light and there will be thunder and lightning, and earthquakes. Mountains will be laid low and valleys made into mountains until the third day, when he shall rise again from the dead. When you see these things, O people of Nephi, repent, or you will be utterly destroyed!"

The mighty voice ceased. The multitude stood staring at Samuel, the dark-skinned Lamanite prophet who stood on the walls of the city. A few days ago he had been banished for his prophecies. It was said he was about to go to his own land when the Lord told him to return. Unable to get into the forbidding city, the walls offered opportunity, and he climbed them and prophesied of the future, crying to all who would listen, "Repent—hear ye Him!"

92

The angry murmur around me swelled to a roar and the air was filled with stones and arrows; but none came near the man on the wall, for the Spirit of the Lord was with him. My bosom was burning with the truth of his words, and I sought out Nephi to be baptized. Those who would not believe sought to bind Samuel, but he leaped down from the wall and was gone.

For five years we faithfully watched and waited for the sign to show that the Son of God was born, but day followed night and night followed day. Many began to believe that the time was past for the prophecy to be fulfilled, and the wicked set a day on which all who believed Samuel's prophecies would be put to death unless the prophecies were fulfilled.

On the evening of that day, as people wearily trudged their way home from their chores, the sun went down as usual but it was still as bright as day; there was no night. The astonishment of the people was so great that they fell to their faces throughout the land.

I will never forget the joy that encompassed me as the sun came up the next day. It was the day for the Son of God to be born. A new star had arisen, and as I watched the clear sky I marveled that the words of Samuel had at last come to pass.

The next few years are a blur in my memory, for they alternated between periods of peace and war, belief and unbelief. At last our land had peace and we were thankful to God for deliverance, but by the time of the thirtieth year after the birth of God's Son, iniquity had split the people into groups, and laws were meaningless. Nephi continued to preach and prophesy, warning us to repent, casting out devils, and healing the sick.

I am old now. Thirty-three years have passed away since the star in the sky and the night that did not grow dark heralded the news that Jesus was born. According to the words of Samuel the time is at hand for the second sign—that of Jesus' death. I may not live to see that great and terrible day, for my heart is heavy that so many will not listen and repent. Again there is argument and disputation that the predicted time is past, and I am weary of it all.

As I sit here musing over the years I can see a strange cloud formation up the valley. It seems to be encompassing the whole sky and darkness is falling. Strange—I hadn't realized it was so late. The world is becoming dark, much as the people's hearts and spirits have become. Suddenly the truth bursts upon me in full force. . . . It is the sign of Christ's death, and the world is in chaos!

* * *

There was excitement in the air that beautiful day in the Land Bountiful. We had gathered there about the temple, which lay glistening in the sun, and were sharing our experiences of those terrible three days without light of any kind. Even the trembling of the earth and groanings of the people could not drown out that powerful voice which proclaimed the destruction of cities and how all but the more righteous had been buried in the earth, carried away by whirlwinds, and destroyed because they would not hear Him.

I listened to my neighbors giving praise to God with a dull sense of the inevitable, for I knew that during those shattering three days I had gone mad.

The madness began the second night of the awful blackness. No candle could be lit because of the intensity of the gloom, yet before my eyes opened a scene I could not in my wildest imagination have conjured up. I could plainly hear the wailing, of both men and the elements, and the thunder crashed around me, so I knew I was awake. . . . Yet how could I have been?

Before me was a courtroom. A foreigner with the emblems of kingship on him was washing his hands in a bowl and saying, "I find no fault in this man. I wash my hands of this affair. . . . It is your responsibility." With a wave of his hand toward the priests standing there he indicated that the figure in the tattered robe should be taken away.

"Do you see?" I whispered to my comrade, clutching his sleeve.

"See!" he exclaimed. "No one sees in this pit of blackness!"

Yet even as he spoke the scene in front of me changed. I saw the man carrying a heavy cross to a hillside. People were jeering and spitting upon him, and he stumbled and fell. The blood from a crown of thorns streamed down his face. In frozen silence I saw the Roman soldiers nail him to the cross he had carried, and mount over his head the sign, "King of the Jews." They taunted him, saying, "If you are God's son, save yourself!"

The sky grew dark over the hillside and his final words, "It is finished," rang through the gathering gloom. The winds howled, the earth rocked, and the night was blacker than ever, yet I had beheld these things with my own eyes. Sweat covered my body as I strove to peer past the curtain of darkness that had descended. Only the ebony night met my gaze.

When the dreadful three days were over, only a few of us were left, and we made our way to the temple at Bountiful. Always I inquired of those I met, "Did you see anything that terrible night?" but the answer was the same, "Nothing."

At last I asked no more, for people were watching me suspiciously and the truth was confirmed within me. No one else had seen those unbelievable events, the meaning of which I knew not, nor did I dare even to ponder over them too much. . . . I was mad. Small wonder; to have lived those hours would bring madness to anyone.

My memories were suddenly interrupted by a voice. I looked around, but no one seemed to have spoken. Again it came, soft yet piercing to my very heart, and then a third time. I raised my eyes to heaven and saw a man in white descending even as the voice spoke once more: "Behold my beloved Son, in whom I am well pleased, in whom I have glorified my name; hear ye him."

Of all the multitude, no one spoke a word. I felt petrified. As the stranger stretched forth his hands saying, "I am Jesus Christ," with one accord we fell to the ground. I lay there, unable to grasp all that was happening. Jesus spoke. The sound was like no other voice I had heard as he told us to come thrust our hands into his side and feel the nail prints in his hands and feet.

One by one all went forward until at last only I remained. Hardly daring to lift my eyes I touched his side. Then drawn by an irresistible power I looked at the jagged scars, the bruised hands, and at last into his face. As I gazed my madness lifted, for it was the face of the One I had beheld in those dreadful hours of his crucifixion.

AND A LITTLE CHILD
SHALL LEAD THEM

The shadows of night still clung to the corners of our humble room when I heard my little son say, "Mother, is it time?" Opening my eyes I saw him standing by my bedside in his tunic, shivering in the chilly morning air. His hand was patting my face and his sightless gaze was turned toward me.

"Hurry, child, into bed before you take cold," I scolded, and quickly drawing him under the blankets with me I held his little body close. "We must wait until the sun rises," I told him. "Go back to sleep."

With a radiant smile he closed his eyes and was soon asleep once more, but sleep for me had fled. What would this day bring, I wondered. We had waited long for the Master to come and today we would behold him with our own eyes. A spasm of pain crossed my face as I thought of the perfect faith of my little son Jason. Would the Master restore his sight? For seven years he had been unable to see; now he was counting so much on Jesus healing him. I knew in my heart that his faith was greater than my own, for even though I too knew Jesus could heal him, I was not sure that he would.

I thought of the day when Jason had run home from the village crying, "Mother! Timothy can walk! He said Jesus put his hand on the twisted leg and it grew straight. I felt the leg and Timothy leaped in the air and shouted!" He hesitated a moment then said, "We must go find Jesus and he will make me see. Have you not told me how he loves children? We must go find him!"

Looking into his eager face I could not bear to dim the joy shining there. "Yes, Jason, we must find him," I slowly replied. Now as I held him close to me I wondered. What if the crowd is too large? What if Jason is not healed? Almost regretfully I remembered my promise to find Jesus. Yet what else could I have done? To have denied the child this chance would have broken his carefully taught faith.

"May we truly find you," I whispered in prayer as Jason stirred in my arms.

"Is it time, Mother?" he asked.

"Yes, my son, it is time."

I cannot remember ever seeing so beautiful a morning as that on which we started out to find Jesus. Jason had asked me to "tell him a color," the game we so often played, and I tried to describe the scenes for him.

"The sky is blue and clear," I said. "There are fat white clouds here and there. The grass is green and since it rained last night, the whole world looks like it has been washed. I can see the shining river winding among the trees and there are flowers everywhere along the road. Old Aaron's donkey is trying to eat them but Sarah keeps him going!" I went on to describe the many travelers following behind us, for they too were going along that same road to find Jesus. Those who were sick and old and could not walk were riding donkeys or being carried on litters. It was a strange feeling, leading the members of that procession to find Jesus. The degrees of faith shown in their faces were varied—yet all were on their way to him.

At last we came to the open field where he stood. I could hardly believe my eyes. There must have been well over two thousand people gathered around him. My heart sank. How could I ever get Jason close enough to ask for help?

One by one we settled ourselves on the ground and listened to the words he spoke.

"What does he look like, Mother?" Jason whispered and with a catch in my breath I replied, "He is straight and beautiful; his face is full of love." Strange how across the crowd his face shone clearly even to those of us on the outside edge.

When he had finished speaking he cast his eyes around the multitude and saw the tears upon our faces, brought by the beauty of his words. "Have you any sick? . . . Bring them to me," he said and I saw the lame, the blind, the leprous, and the deaf touched by him. They made their way back to their families shouting with joy.

I need not have worried about getting Jason to him, for the people went in an orderly manner, making way for one another until all could reach the Master.

"Bring the children," he commanded, and the children surged forward, seating themselves in a circle around him. One by one he touched and blessed them. Jason was the last, and when Jesus placed his hand on my son's head, the lad's cry of gladness mingled with Jesus' words, "Behold your little ones!"

I looked and at first all I could see was Jason, with his eyes wide in comprehension of all about him. He was pointing, spellbound, into the heavens. I raised my own eyes. There the heavens opened and I too could see what my son had first seen. Angels were descending from heaven with fire, until they surrounded the little ones with fire. And the angels ministered to the children.

My heart beat with gladness and I could hardly restrain myself. When at last Jason ran to me through the crowd, I clutched him to my breast. "Mother, don't cry," he said. "I can see now—don't cry."

"These are tears of happiness," I said and smiled. His answering smile was as holy and beautiful as the angels' countenances had been.

"It is a miracle," I whispered softly as we looked at our friends. No longer was there blindness or twisted limbs or pain. Sorrow had momentarily departed from the earth, for each one there had been touched by Jesus.

Once again I looked into my little son's trusting face. "You see, Mother," he explained patiently, "all we had to do was to come to Jesus. He did the rest." I knew that the key to the future was in Jason's words. Our part was to come to Jesus. . . . He did the rest.

THE PLOW IN THE FURROW

"Read to me a bit, won't you, Mother?" I asked. My dear wife smilingly got the big Bible from the shelf. It seemed to fall open of its own accord to the ninth chapter of Luke, the sixty-first and sixty-second verses.

The sunlight filtered in through the open door to light up her silvery hair as she crossed to the rocking chair next to mine and began to read, " 'And another also said, Lord, I will follow thee; but let me first go and bid them farewell who are at my house. And Jesus said unto him, No man having put his hand to the plow and looking back is fit for the kingdom of God.' "

She quietly closed the book and reached her hand to me. The bonds of our love had never been so strong as in that moment, and in the silence that followed, our hearts reached back over the years. The words she had spoken were dear to us both, for it had been a plow in a furrow that had glorified my life that spring day so many years ago.

From the time I had been a young boy my life had been one of searching to meet the Master. My parents were God-fearing people who taught me to respect the Almighty, but the stirrings within my heart called for more than respect; I longed for the Christ of the New Testament who worked in people's lives and guided them in love.

He didn't seem to be found in the services we so faithfully attended. Often I slipped away to a favorite spot along the stream where he seemed nearer to me than in the churches. I could hear the water rippling over the mossy stones, watch the squirrels chasing each other along the logs, and always a peace beyond description would fill my heart and mind.

One morning when I arrived at my "stronghold," as I called it, I was disturbed to find someone already there. It seemed an intrusion, for no one had previously sought out the place of beauty I had labeled my own. I crept closer to see who had dared climb the steep hill and follow the nearly indiscernible path through the brambles, then stopped short. There on her knees beside my brook was the most beautiful girl I had ever seen. She was not praying; she was looking up through the lacy foliage to the clear blue sky and smiling. Her face glowed, and she seemed to see beyond the white clouds overhead.

I could not take my eyes from her face as she suddenly called out, "Good morning, God—what a glorious day you have made!" I gasped, for never had I heard anyone speak so. At the slight sound she whirled around, wide-eyed, and looked straight at me. Scrambling to her feet she started to run, but I called, "Wait!" and she paused. I had once seen a deer poised in flight the same way. Slowly I approached her.

From the bottom of my heart the questions came. "How did you find God that way? I want to know him as you do." Strange words to be spoken that early morning there in the woods, yet the spirit of my longing crept through to her, and she came to where I stood.

"If with all your heart you want to know him, you too will find him," she began, then went on to tell me she believed God spoke to people today. She had just moved to Fayette from near Palmyra, New York, and had slipped out very early that morning to talk with God for a few moments before the busy day of unpacking should begin.

My halting questions showed the searching I had done and she went on to tell me a story so unusual in content, yet so beautiful, that I was amazed. She told me of a young neighbor, Joseph Smith, whom an angel had visited, and how he had waited for several years until God showed him what his work should be. Her family and the Smith family had

106

always been close friends, but when he gave up farming for some mysterious book he said was being copied from golden plates an angel had given him, her parents forbade any of the children to go near the Smith place.

Her eyes filled with tears while she was speaking, and she quietly finished. "For the first time in my life I disobeyed my mother and father. I knew that what Joseph taught was true. The churches today do not teach of God's wondrous love, or all of his word, just as the angel said. I believe God's church will be restored."

Here then was the answer to all the prayers I had offered, the way that Christ himself had taught. I felt no doubt that these things were true, for a spirit of longing filled my breast, like the burning of a fire.

Suddenly I realized that the sun was high in the sky and both of us had daily chores to attend to. "Where can I see you again, and when?" I asked, for the feeling between us was so pure and holy it seemed incredible that we had just met. I knew I must see her again, not only for her company but to hear of the experiences she had had.

The days and weeks that followed were unsurpassed joy, and our courtship was filled with wonder and God's blessings. The one sad drop in our cup of happiness was that her parents would not allow us to speak of Joseph Smith and his experiences, but we trusted that in time God would touch their hearts until they too believed. Of all the beautiful memories the one most clear and most cherished is that moment when the minister looked gravely into our faces and asked, "Sarah, do you take James to be your lawful wedded husband?" and her ringing answer was heard throughout the little church, "I do!"

We had a tiny cottage near the prosperous Whitmer farm where I worked, and never has there been such a blessed life as we shared. As soon as the daily work was ended, Sarah would read to me in the firelight. God's Spirit was with us. Sarah accepted unquestioningly all the things God gave. It was a little harder for me. I still had far to go in my search for complete faith.

A great longing had come over me to see a miracle. Sarah scolded a bit. "James, can you not see our very lives are miracles?"

"Yes, my dear, I believe this and yet. . . ." My voice would trail off as my thoughts turned to the thrilling days when Christ touched the lives of the multitudes.

In early spring of 1829 Father and Lucy Smith stopped over in the Whitmer home. Sarah was overjoyed to see them and as I heard again the story of his son Joseph, my bosom burned with its truth. The Whitmers also were anxious to know more as they were acquainted with Oliver Cowdery, who even now was writing for Joseph as he translated the golden plates.

A few weeks later Oliver wrote asking if they might come to the Whitmer home, for once more persecution had started against them there in Harmony. The Whitmers welcomed them with open arms and David was to go for them as soon as he could; but the spring plowing had to be finished before he could leave.

"Let me finish," I begged, but he shook his head saying, "No, we'll work on it and as soon as it is completed I will go."

That evening as I put away the tools I looked over the fields, noting the vast expanse remaining, and uneasiness filled my breast. It would be at least a week before we could finish, and Oliver had written that persecution was growing daily. Shaking my head sadly, I determined to work every minute it was light enough to see.

The next morning just before daybreak I quietly made my way to the Whitmer home. I would get the tools out and be ready to start that huge field the very moment the first ray of the sun brightened the gloom. I felt for the plow but I couldn't seem to find it. Yet I was sure I remembered exactly where I'd left it the previous night. Perhaps David had moved it. I felt further, but could discover no plow. Not knowing what to do next, I stepped from the toolshed just as the sun in a glorious blaze burst over the horizon. I looked, then rubbed my eyes, and looked again. The field that had lain untouched last night had been plowed! Ahead of me it stretched in the sunlight, ready for the planting. There in a furrow close to a small unfinished portion was the missing plow.

The glory within me outshone the brilliant sunshine as I shouted, "David!" Within moments the Whitmer family had surrounded me and were silently gazing at the field. "Hurry!" I cried. "We can finish quickly and you can leave for Harmony." By the time breakfast was ready, the work was done and David was ready to leave on the journey to bring Oliver and the Smiths to the Whitmer home.

The days, weeks, and years that followed were ones of joy interspersed with pain—joy at the wonderful blessings of God, pain at the persecution. Yet Sarah and I had come unscathed through it all. Often on this new little farm, so far from Fayette and the quiet glade where we met so long ago, Sarah and I walk at the end of day to another quiet spot and kneel to give thanks for God's goodness to us.

* * *

The sound of her voice now recalled me to the present. "James," she said, "so often over the years I have wondered. Why wasn't the whole field plowed that night? Why was a portion left undone?"

I hesitated for a moment, then spoke. "It has never been fully explained, dear one, yet in my heart I feel it was a symbol. Just as the work started by Jesus on the cross of Calvary must be finished by those who love him, so must the field be plowed by those who would serve."

The pressure of the little hand in mine tightened as she softly replied, "I believe you are right, James. If He had done it all for us, it would have been too easy just to continue to leave it to him. He wants us to start at the exact spot where he left off and continue until the work is finished."

Quick tears sprang to my eyes at her words "the exact spot where he left off." "Yes, my dear," I answered. "And to show us where that very place is, he leaves the plow in the furrow."

THE SCOFFER

The night was dark and cold as we cautiously made our way to the Smith home. We waited until all were in place surrounding the house before approaching the front door. No light appeared and all inside was still.

"Now!" came the cry, and with the strength of wild men we hurled ourselves through the door. In the flickering torchlight Mrs. Smith was sitting up in bed, wide-eyed as we dragged "the Prophet" from the covers, still half asleep, and into the darkness. As the door slammed shut behind us the high thin wail of a baby rose in the night air. In spite of our mission a feeling of shame rose within me for a moment but was soon forgotten as we hurried through the woods with our burden to meet those who had gone for Sidney Rigdon.

It was a strange scene there in the woods that raw March evening. Justice was being carried out. For weeks and months feelings had been growing about this new religion—"Mormon" it was called. This man Joe Smith was the subject of much discussion. Even before he arrived with his family stories had drifted out from back East of the claims he made. Why, it was said he saw angels; one of them had supposedly helped him dig in the earth and out popped plates of gold with strange writing on them! The whole thing had been laughable until he had gone too far. He claimed God told him that all existing churches were wrong, that he should join none of them, and that God would "restore" his church to earth.

Never had our peaceful little town been so shaken. We had many different beliefs of God, but what did it matter? We were all on our way to heaven. Now this man comes along with stories of visions and God talking to him, telling him we are all wrong. It was just too much!

Bit by bit the resentment had spread, a muttered word here, a scowl there, and tonight was the climax. . . . This blasphemer and others like him would be taught a lesson. Let him go back to his farming and forget this madness. Perhaps we were even doing him a service, for does not the Bible teach that men must be made humble? These were the thoughts racing through my head as we readied the tar and finished our self-appointed chastening. Rigdon apparently had been taken elsewhere for his lesson.

When it was all over we left to make our way home quietly so we would not be suspected of this

113

evening's work should Smith get home sooner than planned. As I silently crept through the forest the wild spirit of elation left me and I was tired—bone tired. My whole system cried out in relief. It was over and the town could go back to its usual daily activity with no more interference.

By the time I had washed the bits of tar from my hands and wearily climbed into bed, I was exhausted. Falling into a deep sleep I was awakened by a light in the room and a dark shape against the door.

"Who goes there?" I demanded, and a whisper echoed in the stillness, "What have you done to my servant?" Then the shadow shifted and was gone. Frozen with disbelief I lay in bed watching as the light faded. I was still staring at the spot many hours later when the gloom preceding dawn began to lift and day arrived.

Forcing myself to arise and go about the morning chores in bright daylight quieted my racing mind. The memory of what I had decided must have been a dream became dim. At breakfast my wife commented, "My, how restless you were last night. You kept me awake half the night with your moaning and threshing about." I knew by her manner that she had seen nothing unusual.

Before we had finished our meal a knock

sounded at the door and shivering in the damp March morning air was a small neighbor boy. "Please, ma'am," he said to my wife, "you know about herbs and such. Could you come? The little twins the Smiths adopted are awful sick. They have measles and last night when some bad men took Mr. Smith away the night air got on them. They think they're going to die."

Wordlessly I watched the stricken look cross my wife's face even as she hurried for cloak and bonnet. We had lost our only child just a few months before, and the scars ran deep. "I'll stay until they're better," she whispered. With tears glistening in her eyes, she followed the small boy across the field.

Shrugging off the feeling of remorse that had started to gnaw within me I was surprised to hear another knock at the door and found a comrade of the night before standing there. With a furtive air he slipped into the kitchen and told me Joseph Smith planned to preach that morning and for appearance's sake it would be well for us to be there, especially with the news of the Smith children's turn for the worse.

In stunned disbelief I stared at him, even while nodding my head. He seemed to have difficulty meeting my eye, hurriedly backed out the door, and was gone.

I stood at the open doorway, heedless of the cold air rushing in, and wondered what kind of man this "Prophet" could be—to be tarred one night and continue his preaching the next morning! A strange feeling was stirring within me, a mixture of admiration and disgust for this man who had not learned his lesson but would face the very crowd who had tormented him. Was he a fool? or . . . unbidden the memory of my "dream" returned. What had the whisperer said? "What have you done to my servant?"

I found my huge frame shaking and I slammed the door shut. But I could not shut out the memories of the night before. I recalled the look on Mrs. Smith's face, the cry of the child, and the scene by torchlight as we had poured the tar over Smith, taunting him with, "If you're a prophet, why don't you call on your God to save you?" Suddenly the similarity of our wording to that of the Jews at the crucifixion struck me. They too had thought they were stamping out blasphemy, yet how wrong they had been. Could we also actually be persecuting a servant of God? A third time I seemed to hear the whisper, "What have you done to my servant?"

"Be still!" I shouted to the empty kitchen. The words echoed back to me from every corner of the room, but my heart was not still at all.

* * *

When I arrived at the meeting place, I studiously avoided nearing any of the participants of the previous night's episode and took a place off to one side where I might go unnoticed. A hymn was sung and then "the Prophet" rose and walked slowly to the front. He looked ill, and great welts of red marred his usually smooth countenance, but there was nothing in his manner of resentment, or hate, or even of fear. It was as if he were surrounded by an invisible wall of protection from which he need fear no more.

I have heard prayers many times in my life, but never a prayer like that. I don't remember what his text was, or whether he even quoted the actual scripture, but all through that service the words rang in my mind, "Saul, Saul, why persecutest thou me?" It beat into my brain like a hammer and I became physically weak.

Now I was listening to Smith's story, for a spirit of truth attended its telling that could not be shut out. He told of his experiences as a young boy, how God had spoken to him, how a light appeared at his bedside, and an angel spoke to him. Here he

117

paused for a moment and I suddenly thought, Saul saw a light; this man claims to have seen a light, a light by his bedside. Just as at my bedside last night.

Smith went on to tell of his growing up years and his efforts to follow God, and strange as it seems, I knew it was true. He closed by saying that any who would repent of their sins would be forgiven and that there would be a baptismal service that afternoon for any who would believe and repent.

Avoiding the knowing grins of my comrades I rushed away from the Presence that had attended that meeting. I knew that in another moment I would follow the two who had gone forward requesting baptism and throw myself at the Prophet's feet, begging forgiveness of him and of God. I realized now the terrible crime I had committed the night before, in the name of Christianity—I, who had always in my own way served God diligently. Then I realized the greatest error of it all: I had served God in my own way, but not in His. God forgive me, what had I done?

The elusive March sunlight had chosen to shine forth for the baptismal service that afternoon. I hung to the back of the crowd, wishing with all my heart I could be with the two slowly entering the water, and knowing it could not be so. The Prophet raised his hand. "Having been commissioned of Jesus Christ, I baptize you in the name of the Father, the Son, and the Holy Ghost. Amen." With my heart breaking from remorse I turned to slip away when Joseph looked into the crowd assembled.

"Are there others here who believe and wish to be baptized for the remission of their sins?" he asked, and those kind eyes seemed to gaze straight into mine. I will never remember just how I responded, but within seconds I was kneeling in front of him, crying out for forgiveness, that he didn't know what I had done, and confessing my sins to God and the people there.

"God knows, and that is enough," he replied, but somehow I felt that he too knew and forgave. As the waters of baptism closed over me, I again saw the figure that had haunted me the past hours. . . . The hands were outstretched and the shadows receded until I could catch a glimpse of the face of our Master.

As I left the water, hands were placed upon me and I knew I too would be spreading the good news. My first thought was to hurry to my wife, but no . . . there was something I must do even before that.

My former comrades appeared stunned that afternoon as one by one I sought them out and tried to share with them what had happened to me. Fear, pity, hatred, and amazement greeted me as I spoke, but disbelief was uppermost in their expressions and I suspect they thought I had gone mad.

The days that followed were difficult. When little Joseph died it was a greater blow to me than to the Smiths. I knew Joseph and God had forgiven me, but I could not yet forgive myself. The only comfort I could find those days was in reading of Paul and his struggles after he had persecuted the Christians and had then found God.

Time passed and my wife and I also became targets of the bitterness surrounding the "Mormon" movement. Being a man of action I had plunged wholeheartedly into telling the beloved story, and many of my former friends now became bitter enemies. We lived from day to day never knowing what new persecution was ahead, yet we were blessed. Because I had been forgiven so much, I learned to forgive many times over in return, until even the bitterest persecution provoked no malice. God had firmly planted hope and complete trust in one who had persecuted his prophet for bringing the very message that at last changed the heart of the scoffer.

NIGHT OF WONDER

The waves beat against the sides of the ferry and sleet poured down. Dry-eyed I turned for a last look at the shore I was leaving. The scene meeting my eyes would have melted the stoniest heart, for there on the banks of the great Missouri River was wretched humanity. Great piles of furniture and clothing, soaked through by the snow and sleet; families searching for one another; children crying in the wilderness—these were God's chosen people.

I could bear no more. I turned to face across the rolling waters, but the scene was the same. There in the cottonwoods the men were trying to put things into a semblance of order. A few had provisions, some boxes and chests, but many like myself had been lucky to escape with only the clothes on their backs.

My mind flashed back to happier days, before the terrible persecution began. Joshua and I had a small cabin there in Independence. He was a government hunter, who furnished meat for the settlements farther west. He regretted the necessity of being gone so much but his contract would soon run out and he would not renew it. Instead he

121

planned to farm the five acres we had bought on which our cabin stood. We would keep chickens and of course some cows for milk.

In spite of my despair a slow warmth filled me as I thought of the moment I had told Joshua, "We must have a milk cow—babies need milk."

He stared at me for a moment, not comprehending, then with a whoop of joy swung me across the cabin floor. "You mean you . . . I . . . we . . ." he stammered, his face shining.

"Yes," I smiled. "We are going to have a son." Even then I was sure it would be a boy, despite the four years of marriage when no babies had come. We had begun to wonder if we could have a family, so this news was precious to us both.

Joshua had been disturbed by the rumors afloat and the trouble in various areas surrounding us. When he was ready to leave on his last hunting trip, he held me close. "I will be back by Thanksgiving," he said soberly, looking deep into my eyes.

"And our son will be here just in time for Christmas," I reassured him. "Don't worry, Joshua, if I need anything I'll ring the bell." He had strung a wire and bell along the fence posts between us and the Joneses, our nearest neighbors.

Doubt still lingered in his eyes but with a final "Be careful," he was gone. Something in the dejected set of his shoulders as he turned away filled my eyes with tears, but brushing them aside I hurried about finishing the kitchen work and made ready for bed.

I had been asleep a very short time when I heard pounding on the front door. Snatching a dressing gown from the chair I threw wide the door to admit Mr. Jones, our neighbor. "Faith, you must come quickly! Don't stop for anything except to dress warmly. The militia is rounding up the Saints, but there is a wild element who are burning and looting. Come quickly, my dear friend."

I numbly obeyed his instructions and with a parting look about the cozy room we loved so well started out the door. "Wait," said Mr. Jones. "You must cover your head," and he snatched a bundle of white from the table.

"Oh, that is for my baby," I cried. "I will find a shawl."

The sound of horses' hooves grew nearer. "There is no time," my good friend insisted. "The Saints in Clay County will welcome and help you . . . and us all," he added.

We slipped out the back door. Before we had gone far there was the sound of breaking glass and the smell of burning. I half turned and saw the flames begin, then setting my face forward I looked back no more. When we arrived at the Temple Lot the people were gathering, dazed, wet, unable to grasp what was happening. I heard one woman say, "But this is America; it can't be happening here," . . . but it was.

For three days we camped there in the downpour. I don't know how any of us lived through it but at last on November 7 we were driven to the river and ordered out of Jackson County.

Now I stood waiting to step from the ferry, but into what? I knew I would never again see our little home. When would I see Joshua? I knew he would search until he found me. Would there be a place for us to go, just a little place where we could find peace, and our baby could grow? We had nothing to build with. Finally shrugging off my bitterness I walked from the ferry to a spot beneath the cottonwoods and huddled close to a fire someone had made. It was the first time I had been warm in three days. I unwound the once white cloth from my head, holding it in front of me to dry. I looked at the tiny stitches. It was to have been a blanket for my son and one corner was yet unfinished. My body was racked with sobs, the first tears I had shed, and with a protective motion I thrust the warm cloth under my dress where it also seemed to warm my cold heart a little.

Darkness fell while the last ferry load of people arrived for the night. Those who had provisions prepared food and shared with those of us less fortunate. Mrs. Jones brought me a steaming bowl of broth and gratefully I drank it to the last drop. I had just set down the bowl when without warning a spasm of pain caught me. Mrs. Jones was immediately beside me. "Your baby, dear," she said, even as I cried out, "But it cannot be. It is not time—there is no place for him to be born." I gazed at my surroundings. Rain had once again started pouring down and there was no shelter.

"We will do the best we can, Faith," Mrs. Jones promised, and she did. With other women of the camp she made a place for me beside a fallen log. Pieces of an old carpet were found and the women took turns holding them above me for some protection from the storm.

With a strained smile I said, "Mrs. Jones, our Lord was born in a manger."

Quick tears filled her eyes and she smiled a little. "Yes," she said, "he was. And your son will grow to be one of his servants."

They wrapped my baby in the unfinished blanket I had kept dry next to my heart and covered me with borrowed coats and blankets. The rain had finally stopped. Completely exhausted, I drifted off to sleep with my little son held closely in my arms.

I was awakened by shouting. As I opened my eyes I at first thought it was snowing great white flakes. Everyone in the camp was up and dressed, even the little children, staring into the sky. The heavens were crossed as if with giant fireworks. Great streaks of light followed by tails of fire filled the sky—not one by one, but so many they could not be counted. The whole world was ablaze, and for over half an hour the display continued. Like huge snowflakes they came, disappearing before they reached the ground.

When it was over we gave thanks to God for this sign that he was with his people. My heart overflowed as my baby's lusty cry told of his strength. In spite of the rude surroundings and circumstances of his birth I knew he would grow and become, as Mrs. Jones had said, a servant of God.

Daybreak heralded the arrival of more Saints. The first one to bound off the ferry when it docked was my own Joshua. "I heard of the troubles," he explained, "and the company said I need not finish my contract since it was so nearly completed. I am so glad to find you. I have been out of my mind with worry!"

A thin cry interrupted him and he started back. "What was that?" I folded the edge of the little unfinished blanket so he could see our tiny son. Joshua's hand trembled as he wordlessly looked at me across our baby. There was nothing left to say. This tiny piece of humanity, arriving in the cottonwoods on the banks of the Missouri River, was our symbol of hope for the future. He had no crib, no clothing of his own; only the love of his parents and the spectacular display the heavens had shown on the night of wonder that marked our baby's birth.

THE DEDICATION

I pulled my shawl closer around me as I hurried to the Temple. No one would know my baby was concealed beneath its folds. Hastily I slipped into one of the last available seats. A few moments later the ushers reluctantly closed the doors, for the room was full to overflowing and others stood outside. There were about a thousand people there that day . . . for our beloved Kirtland Temple was being dedicated.

I sat gazing about the large room with its beautiful mullioned windows. I realized that although we had indeed come this day to dedicate the Temple, the real dedication had been in its building. Days of work, sacrifice, and love had erected this monument to God, for in spite of bitter persecution it had continued to rise, calling forth the best of each one. Only short weeks had passed since our women had brought their finest china and glassware to be crushed in the final layer of covering on the exterior walls. Now the gleaming brightness sparkled in the sunshine and could be seen for miles around.

A slight movement of my baby filled me with

panic for a moment. "Be still," I prayed and as he settled down once more I breathed a sigh of relief. The elders had requested that babes in arms not be admitted, for the crowd was large and the services were to be long.

My mind turned to the chain of events leading to this moment. The neighbor who had been planning to care for my baby had rushed in early this morning. "My own children are sick," she said. "I cannot care for your son; he might even catch the illness."

My heart sank as she hurried away. What could I do? My husband had already gone to make preparations for the service and it was too late to find someone else to care for my baby. I looked at him lying there asleep. Surely it would do no harm to tuck him under my shawl. He never cried in church, and he was tiny.

The sight of the glistening white Temple was too much for me. I felt I must be present at its dedication. Now, glancing at my baby's face under the pretext of adjusting my shawl I was happy to find him asleep once more.

It is impossible to find words in which to express the events of that day. The faces of those leading the services glowed with the Spirit of God until they seemed set apart like angels. The words spoken were of deepest thanksgiving, for the completion of our dream was almost unbelievable. So many times we had wondered if this day would ever be. Now around us rose the tangible evidence of God's love and protection.

The day progressed and in the spirit of the hour I had nearly forgotten the sleeping baby. When it seemed that we would be carried away by the very presence of God, each heart overflowing, a voice cried out from the depths of my shawl, "Hosannah to God!" The silvery tones were those of a child. In amazement I threw back the enfolding garment and beheld my son. He had not spoken before—yet even the mouths of babes must paise the Lord. My baby's first words had been to the greatness of God.

The rest of the day's happenings are blurred in my memory. I remember tears streaming down our faces as my husband and I looked at our child. We knew he would be used by God when he was older. It would be our responsibility to see that he was ready when the call should come. Our hands clasped in mutual acceptance of the challenge, and our hearts echoed our baby's first words cried out that wonderful dedication day at Kirtland, "Hosannah to God!"

THE FIERY TRIAL

I Peter 4:12, 13: "Beloved, think it not strange concerning the fiery trial which is to try you, as though some strange thing happened unto you; but rejoice, inasmuch as ye are partakers of Christ's sufferings; that, when his glory shall be revealed, ye may be glad also with exceeding joy."

The words came faintly from the pallid lips of my father. He paused a moment then continued, "Take care of Mother and the little ones, son, and don't let the tragedy of today fill you with bitterness." He raised his head, looked into the sky, and with a glorious look on his face he called out, "Master!" and was gone.

Hot tears filled my eyes and I led my weeping mother away. My own heart was so numb from the events of the last few weeks I could no longer even think clearly. It was all so senseless, so uncalled for! The little group of families living at Haun's Mill troubled no one, but worked hard and minded their own business.

It had been just three weeks since that terrible October afternoon. While the autumn leaves fell in beauty, a mob of about two hundred had ridden into our midst, killing and looting. The women and most of the children ran to the protection of the timber which bordered Shoal Creek, but the few men in camp valiantly attempted to defend our homes and the wagons of the visiting Saints camping with us for a few days.

David Evans ran up a white flag of surrender which the mob answered only with a fresh round of firing. As our men ran from the blacksmith shop they were cut down, then the mob sought out those still alive to finish them, too. Two boys were cruelly shot, one to die immediately, one just last night after three weeks of suffering.

In spite of my father's last words hate rose within me as we buried him. I remembered the other fathers; we had no strength to dig so many graves so we put them in an old dry hole that had been planned for a well.

Two days later the mob returned to take possession of what had been left. They harvested our crops, butchered the hogs and cattle, and left the haunted spot to its widows and orphans who had nowhere to go.

In the late evening following their departure I

crept to the edge of the clearing and gazed at the desolation. The happy, peaceful little spot was complete ruin; all was gone. Since our family lived some distance from town the mob had somehow missed us and we did have a spot of garden left and a cow. In despair I shook my fist at the settlement. How could we ever survive? Winter was even then covering the highest hills with its crown of white. When the others had gone I stood firm. We would not leave—no, we could not—for Father was too badly hurt to be moved. He had appeared dead at first. That is how we were able to drag him home from the edge of the clearing and away from the mob without being discovered. Now he too was gone and I was the only man left in Haun's Mill. . . . I was twelve years old.

I will never understand how we managed to make it through the winter. I was strong and willing but inexperienced. Joey and Sally, the eight-year-old twins, helped all they could. Mary, our five-year-old, took over care of the baby, and my mother was amazing. She kept our family busy, finding things for the children to do in the evenings. "Come, Peter," she would say. "We'll see who can shuck the most corn." Or she would invent some other means by which work could be accomplished yet seem like play.

I often felt her gaze and knew she was concerned about my silence, for in the winter days and hardships I became old. Responsibility had changed me from a laughing, mischievous boy into the man of the family, with no time for merriment.

As the long winter drew to a close, we planned what we should do. "It is too hard for us, Peter," she said quietly. "The children need friends and schooling. We will go away and find other Saints who will help us." I knew she was right. We had no other choice, yet my heart rebelled at being deprived of our home by ruthless men.

On an evening green and beautiful with the first shoots of spring growth, we finished packing our few goods into the old wagon. We had no horse, so Mother said, "You and I must be the horses, Peter." We had decided to start in the evening, when the sun was painting the western sky with a symbol of hope.

We paused at the top of a small rise for one last backward glance. "Look," whispered little Mary. "It's on fire!"

Indeed it appeared so. The ruddy sun had gilded each nook and cranny of the deserted settlement until it looked aflame. The bitterness in my heart threatened to overwhelm me when in the midst of that awful splendor a voice spoke: "Peter, think it not strange concerning the fiery trial, but rejoice! My glory shall be revealed." As I fell to my knees the light moved and one last shaft of sunlight formed a blazing cross above the desecrated, now glorified spot.

With eyes full of all the tears I should have shed during the long hard months now past, I faced forward and looked back no more.

THE ICY BARRIER

I have never seen courage as I saw it today. Often I have wondered about Mrs. Smith, our Prophet's wife, who has gone through so much, and today I met her for the first time.

When the call came that Far West was being attacked I bundled my wife into the big wagon and drove away from all our possessions. It was not the first time we had been driven from our homes, for there is much ill feeling against the Saints here in Missouri.

After several days of traveling we arrived at the banks of the Mississippi River. "Look!" my wife called. "It is solid ice!" There before us lay the great river, helpless in its wintry garb. On the other side lay Illinois where, hopefully, we would find peace.

Along with several others we decided to camp there for the night and cross into Quincy the following day. Soon there were huge fires along the banks, and in spite of the bitter cold day we managed to keep warm if we stayed close to the flames.

It was nearly dark when a lone wagon pulled

into camp. I recognized the driver, Johnathan Holman, a kindly man. With him were a woman and four children, one only a baby.

"Whoa," shouted Johnathan and old Jim and Charley, the horses, stopped their plodding as if glad to rest, as well they might be. It had been a terrible trip in the snow the past days.

As the woman came near our fire to warm herself and her children, Johnathan said, "This is Emma Smith." I looked at the tired face, the shadows under the great brown eyes, and was struck by the beauty shining through all the weariness and despair. Even then her husband Joseph was in Liberty Jail, held on one of the countless charges the persecutors trumped up. She had suffered much, yet the radiance of her spirit was undimmed.

I looked at the baby Alexander, little Frederick, the older children Julia and little Joseph, and thought of this woman's other children, left behind in little graves now mounded with snow. Truly this woman was called of God, even as was her husband.

"Stay and share with us," my wife was pleading. "We haven't much, but you are very welcome."

Mrs. Smith's eyes grew moist. "Thank you, my dear," she replied. Looking at the great sheet of frozen river ahead she went on, "We must go. I am anxious to get across that icy barrier and into Quincy where my children can be cared for." Seeing her determination we said no more, but stood at the edge of the river as they started across.

Brother Holman unhitched Jim and led him to the front of Charley, tying him there. "The wagon won't hold all of us. Be careful, it is very slippery," he warned.

Telling the older children to remain in the wagon, Mrs. Smith picked up the baby and Frederick.

Little Joseph and Julia were frightened. "Let us walk, too," they begged.

"Then hold fast to me," their mother replied.

A great lump filled my throat as we watched the brave little family hesitatingly make their way across what she had termed the "icy barrier." I understood her expression, for it was exactly that—an icy barrier of hate and prejudice against God's people by the other Missouri residents.

"She is very brave," said my wife, standing close beside me.

"Yes," I responded, "and she carries the hope of the gospel with her."

"What do you mean?" she asked.

"I overheard Sister Scott when she gave Mrs.

Smith a strange looking contraption of bags sewed to a band, long enough to be tied around a woman's waist underneath the dress. I feel sure it contains the manuscript of the inspired version of the scriptures which Joseph has been working on."

In awe we again turned our attention to the struggling figures across that glistening expanse. They had reached the Illinois shore and were climbing back into the wagon. In spite of the bitter cold we watched them out of sight.

"I don't see how she does it," my wife said. "Did you see her face? In spite of all the heartbreak she has suffered, her soul shines out in perfect faith that God is over all."

Straining my eyes for a last glimpse of this courageous woman I was silent for a time. The wind was piercing our garments and the cold was intense. Yet through my body poured the warmth that could only be the Holy Spirit.

At last I turned to my own dear wife. She too had gone through much. The sight of her rounded form reminded me that we would be blessed with a child in early summer. I thought of the little children who had so trustingly clung to the mother's skirts across that wide stretch of snow and ice, and my eyes misted.

"If it is a girl," I whispered gently as we turned back to the warmth of our fire, "we will call her Emma." A flash of understanding crossed my wife's face. She put her hand in mine and we returned to our wagon. On the morrow, we too must cross that icy barrier.

CITY BEAUTIFUL

Moonlight streamed down through leafy branches. The wind softly whispered through the trees. In the distance a dog howled and the loneliness of his call struck an answer in my heart. I dropped down beside a broken wall of the ruined temple and gave way to my grief.

It was long after midnight, this quiet hour I had chosen to steal forth from my bed. I had been sleepless, waiting for all to become quiet. Then, in the way of young boys, I had silently crept out my window, running barefooted down the lane and up to the temple.

My mother and father would worry if they knew I was out this time of night, for it was no longer safe for twelve-year-old boys to roam about at night. Since so many had left Nauvoo, attacks on those Saints who remained had increased. Families were robbed of all that was worth stealing, and fear lived in the hearts of all. I was afraid now, but I had to come. Father had told us at supper that we would be leaving at daybreak. "We cannot fight any more," he said, and Mother agreed.

I could not speak. Leave Nauvoo? It was almost

more than I could stand. Wide-eyed I lay until I was able to steal away. I just had to say good-bye to my beloved city.

Now I lay sobbing beside the ruins of the temple. Lightning had partially destroyed it. I remembered the way all of us had worked together; even small boys were allowed to help. Once Joseph Smith himself had guided my hand along the limestone with his. "See?" he had told me. "Together our work becomes easier. One day you will be bigger and then you will help make it easier, too." His smile warmed a small boy's heart and I was proud to carry water and lunches to the men, dreaming of the day I would be working with them to build the temple of God.

No one could even guess how deep my feelings were for this city beautiful, Nauvoo. I could barely remember coming from England in the ship. We had been so sick, and many had died along the way. Weak and tired we had reached Nauvoo, on the Mississippi River. I remembered sighting along the slope to the bluffs overlooking the water and wondering if I had died and gone to heaven.

The people took us in and cared for us until we were strong and able to start a little farm. In spite of all my chores I had time to make friends and, with the other boys, to watch the Nauvoo Legion drilling outside of town—over a thousand members proudly marching. There was the sawmill, with its cheerful whine, and the brick kiln making hundreds of bricks. The swamp that had once been filled with mosquitoes was drained now, and those long sloping paths from bluff to river were made for races. I never won, but the excitement of running along those trails was enough for me.

I remembered the first time our own steamboat pulled into the harbor. "Maid of Iowa" was painted on her side. I thought of my own terrible trip from England and was happy that the people who rode on this ship would not be packed together and sick.

Now, those days were gone forever, and tomorrow we would be leaving. I huddled there on the ground, unable to understand why God would let such things happen to his people. I had overheard Joseph Smith one day telling Sidney Rigdon he wished all the people were as devoted as Mr. Fordham, who was working on the carvings of the big oxen. He felt that the spiritual level of the people should be higher. Their devotion was far less evident than during the building of the Kirtland Temple. Brother Smith felt that the work was being held back to some extent by this.

I didn't understand what he meant, and asked

Mother that evening. She said many of the people were filled with pride and were not humble before God. "Jamie, don't ever forget," she warned. "God wants us to love and trust him just as you do now. That's what he asks us to do, no matter what happens."

Her words didn't mean much then but now they came back to me. "It's hard to trust you, God," I cried out to the sky and friendly stars. "Our prophet is dead and his son Joseph is too young to lead us—those of us who are left." People had gone away to different places. Some were with Brigham Young going West. I had sadly waved good-bye; yet strangely enough, even at that age I knew my father was right in refusing to join the long trek to the Rocky Mountains. He said it was wrong to follow any of the leaders who had taken groups away.

I remembered the face of the Prophet that Sunday afternoon in the grove. Young Joseph sat on the bench beside him. He looked as if he'd rather be down in the grass with the rest of us boys, for he was nearly eleven and one of our best friends.

His father told those gathered there—and it must have been several thousand—that if he were killed or if he died, young Joseph would become our

144

leader and prophet. He continued with his sermon, saying, "My work is nearly done. He will be my successor," and pointed to his son.

My mind flashed back to a few days before. Several of us had climbed a hill and young Joseph had told us how his family had been treated everywhere they lived. Then very solemnly he had told us of the night he spent with his father in Liberty Jail—how his father and Lyman Wight had placed their hands on his head. With tears streaming down his face the Prophet had blessed his son and named him as his successor.

My heart beat faster and I held out my hand to young Joseph. The bonds of children's friendship are strongest when touched by things of God, even when these things are not completely understood.

I just couldn't believe that all those happy hours were gone. Suddenly a rustling in the grass warned me that someone was approaching. Quietly I watched as a familiar figure came into sight around the crumbled wall.

"Joseph," I whispered, as he came closer.

"Jamie!" he cried out in surprise. "Couldn't you sleep either?"

"No," I explained. "We are leaving tomorrow and I just had to come here once more." I hesitated then went on, "What will you do, Joseph?"

His head dropped into his hands. "I don't know," he replied dejectedly. "It is so hard. Mother feels we should stay at least a little longer. Oh, Jamie, what can we do?"

I was filled with pity for my friend who had lost his father and most of his friends. I heard myself repeating my mother's words, "God wants us to love and trust him no matter what happens." Then I added softly, "Joseph, your father did."

He sat up, and although his face was still wet with tears, the slump of hopelessness was no longer there. "Yes, Jamie, he did."

Once more the night was still, once more a dog barked in the distance, but gone was the complete loneliness we had experienced.

"We must go," he said, and we stood up and watched the dawn begin to break. The grassy slope to the stream, the bluffs, the shining river began to take form. We walked down the path to where the trail cut off to the Mansion House.

Turning for a last look I clutched his arm. "Look," I cried, for there above us stood the temple. Early morning mists veiled the broken and

146

unfinished portions; all that could be seen was a beautiful structure, sitting proudly on a hill.

Clasping hands in farewell young Joseph and I looked deep into each other's eyes and again at the dream temple of God rising above us. This then was the parting of ways, the separation of friends. But with that vision above us, it was not the end.

THE CHOSEN ONE

Prologue

The breeze from the open window fluttered the well-mended curtains, then was still. A lazy bumblebee buzzed above the motionless figure lying on the bed, then hurried back outdoors in search of more excitement. The slumberer stirred in his sleep, and opened his eyes. Shaking his head in amazement he appeared bewildered—and no wonder! Gone were the familiar Mansion House walls of his Nauvoo home. The warm May sunshine was the same, yet it shone on scenes unfamiliar to him in spite of his twenty-one years.

Before him lay a large city, busy offices, crowded streets. People bustled to and fro, and he knew he was one of them; he saw himself as a man of prestige, caught up in important affairs.

The scene slowly disappeared, to be replaced by another. Rolling farmlands stretched in front of him as far as he could see. The land was peopled by kindly folk, gentle and intelligent. Peace and unity permeated the land. Again he felt a part of this picture.

The rolling hills faded from view. His bedroom walls were before him, yet he knew one of the roads must be taken. Only he could choose the road, and once taken, there would be no turning back.

* * *

With anxious hearts we waited. The time seemed long since our brothers Gurley and Briggs had started their journey to Nauvoo. I remembered well the night before they left. We had gathered for prayer that they might fulfill their mission. Both elders bore testimony that God had made known to them that they should go to Young Joseph and ask him to lead this faithful remnant of Christ's own church. Evidence of the Spirit was strong, and our hearts burned within us as we received witness to the truthfulness of their words.

I recalled the journey of so many years before when, homeless and destitute, we had banded together and moved to Wisconsin, naming our settlement Zarahemla. We had determined to keep the pure teachings of Jesus, and in spite of the desolate area we occupied, we had love for one another and peace. It seemed a long time since 1844 and the death of the Prophet. His son was a

149

man now, and of age to carry out the designation of his father—that of prophet, seer, and revelator to the church.

Those who had been too young to remember the Prophet blessing his son as his successor never tired of hearing stories from the past and of the persecution we had experienced. I am an old man now, and have earned the right to sit in the sun and spin tales of those early days. My fondest dream, though, is not of the past but once again to know that God's chosen prophet is at the head of the restored church.

The waiting has grown even harder since Brother Gurley returned. He and Brother Briggs were astounded that Young Joseph had greeted them with some hostility. After talking with him, their understanding grew. He had been approached by representatives of many factions, whose teachings had departed from the truth. He could not and would not accept the responsibility we offered until he learned from God himself that the calling was true. Brother Briggs accordingly decided to stay near Nauvoo, working and preaching, for he did not wish to return without Joseph's decision to come to the church as leader.

I often wondered at the trials Young Joseph must be having, sorting out truth from falsehood,

God's teachings from man's preachings. "Which church is right?" would be his query, as it had been his father's.

Many months would pass before the extent of his questioning and testing was fully known, yet my heart cried out to God on his behalf: "Guide the laddie, dear Father, and grant him wisdom."

At one time Young Joseph seriously considered going West to Utah to clear his father's name. Heeding his father's counsel he literally "asked of God." His answer came in a luminous cloud which enveloped him with radiance, and his question was answered: "The light in which you stand is greater than theirs."

Following the loss of his beloved child, Joseph again began to consider just what God wanted of him. He gave deep thought to what it was he should do, and his experiences from the past rushed over him. The blessings of his father at Liberty Jail and in Nauvoo and the vision of that warm day in May so long ago returned to him. He remembered the peacefulness of those rolling farmlands, the singleness of heart among the people, the joy because there was no sin.

"It is the kingdom of God!" he whispered. His thoughts turned to our little group at Zarahemla who, in spite of hardship, now numbered nearly a thousand. We were a beginning, the foundation, preaching the truth of the gospel by our daily lives, sacrificing gladly to carry out God's work.

And so I saw the reorganization of the Church of Jesus Christ of Latter Day Saints. On April 6, 1860, just thirty years after the original church had been organized, Young Joseph took his place before us. My heart overflowed and tears ran unheeded and unchecked down my face. Joseph spoke in the simplest and humblest way, and his face shone with love as he quietly told us he would give his all in service to the Master.

I will never forget the look he carried; it was that of a man with a dream, and the eternal vision to make it come true. My joy was complete. . . . My laddie, who had been chosen, had now chosen his road and was ready to serve that the kingdom of God might come again on earth.

THE QUEST

"I have a right to live my own life! Why should I be shackled to someone else's ideas of what's right and wrong? What's the big deal about religion anyway? I believe in God and Christ, but why do I have to go around talking about it all the time? Just because I'm a preacher's kid everyone expects me to be really great. I'm tired of it. I want to get out in the world and see for myself. . . . I want to get out and really live!"

Like voices from the past the impassioned words poured from Jim, the teen-age son of one of the elders. I could see his feelings echoed in the faces of Sally, Joe, Pete, and the rest of the camp's youth class gathered at the edge of the lake for early morning worship. They were mostly church youth, with a sprinkling of visitors mixed in, and I was teaching their class. For several days I had seen this spirit of rebellion building against the "pattern" of religion as they understood it. Today it had erupted. Yet beyond the boy's honesty of expression I could see honest searching, a fear that religion was merely "preaching." These teen-agers were attempting to discover if there was any substance to what they had been taught.

Closing my eyes for a moment I thought of the prayers I had offered on their behalf. There was a steady feeling of urgency about what I must do. I had considered it before, yet rationalized my way out of it. But in Jim's words I found an appeal that would not be denied by my personal hesitancy to bare my soul to these young people. Clasping my hands behind my back to still their trembling, and putting down the rush of pain inside me, I faced Jim squarely and began to speak in an unnatural voice things I had vowed to put behind me forever.

"You want to get out in the world where you'll be free, Jim. You want to really live! Let me tell you what it's like—that big, wonderful, exciting world you long for, away from God. You can't name one area of it I haven't explored. When it comes to all the paths offered . . . I've been there."

A ripple of surprise ran through the group, and the cynical look on Jim's face lifted for a moment as I went on.

"Most of you have known me only a short time. In many ways I am still a stranger to you. You've known me since I let Christ scoop me up out of the mud at the bottom of life and bring me back up that path you are so anxious to take. It's a lot easier to walk down that road than it is to walk back. Once I had a quest, and for ten years I lost it . . . ten years without God! It surprises you to hear these things about me, doesn't it?"

I hesitated a moment. The group was staring at me in rapt attention. Once again that strange, unnatural voice that I knew was my own took up the story.

"I was just like you, Jim, ready to set the world on fire for a cause. When I was baptized I thought I had that cause, and my quest began. I felt that God asked people to walk as his companions, without the daily troubles, with joy and happiness. I searched for this life for days, weeks, months, years—a shining dream which I was sure could be found if only I looked long enough. I looked to those around me—but over the years they had allowed the pressures of life to dim their vision of simple trust and humility. The peace and joy I sought were not in their homes, nor in their lives."

Noting the nod of heads I continued. "There were those who said my quest was too idealistic, and that I was not old enough or wise enough to challenge them. 'Just do the best you can,' they said. I couldn't accept this. 'Do the best you can'? Was that all there was to my longings for a walk with God? I too began to doubt. I stopped attending church. With me it was all or nothing. I wouldn't settle for second best, a God who fit only in the spare corners of people's lives. Needing a replacement, like thousands of others, I recklessly tried out all the thrills, rushing through days and nights—and finding only loneliness and emptiness. Years passed. I had tried it all, and there was nothing left. Life was something to be endured. I had been hurt, but found if you don't allow yourself to care, no one can hurt you. So I built a wall around myself, brick by brick, cementing it with indifference, sealing it with scorn, until the world was shut out and I was 'safe!'

"This was my life for ten years. The eager boy had turned into a bitter man, determined to be untouched by the human race.

"One night those empty, lonely, wasted years overwhelmed me and in spite of my 'wall' I found myself crying out, 'Who am I? Where am I going? Does anything matter, or does anyone care?' The shadows of my room mocked me. 'What? You? You are inside a wall just where you longed to be, yet you cry for mercy? Why is it you ask for something other than that which you have achieved?'

"I don't know—perhaps I fell asleep from exhaustion—but suddenly the room brightened and in the place of the mocking shadows stood a person. He took me by the hand and led me over my entire life until I thought I would die from the pain of the unproductive years I had spent. Then he reminded me that the object of my quest had been, love, understanding, reality, built on simple trust in God. 'You see,' he explained, 'you looked too far, and made it too hard. God is within you if you will only seek him there.'

"The dark room was once more with me and he was gone. I found tears on my face, the first I had shed in years. I had been given a second chance."

There was a hush over the group by the lake. Jim's head was in his hands, and the tears on my face were reflected in some eyes. Sally whispered, "We didn't know . . . we just didn't know."

In a quieter tone now I spoke, "Jim, in spite of that wonderful experience it's still been a long, hard road back. Going down those paths is so easy, but they're all dead ends. Coming back up them is a different story. Many times I've stumbled and fallen over the very rocks in the road on which I once stood laughing. Even though it has been several years I'm still tearing down that wall I built around me. I had to go back to the exact spot where I left off, pick up, and start again.

"You asked why it's such a big deal, and why

talk about it if you believe in Christ. I'll tell you why I have to do this: I was one of the lucky ones. How many of your friends have you seen who lost faith in their dream, never to return? It isn't easy to relive these experiences or to speak of them. But when I had no hope, nothing, Christ came to me. He led me back step by step. Can I live my life without speaking of him, my best Friend? If someone did that for you—literally saved your life—would you tell people about it? I feel that's exactly what he's done for me."

After a long moment Jim got to his feet. His eyes met mine in a long, clear look as he gripped my hand. "Thank you," he said very simply. With one accord the little group moved quietly up over the hill, each struggling with his own feelings.

I dropped to my knees, physically spent. "Oh, God, I didn't think I could ever voice these feelings."

The silence of the little glade was broken only by the ripples in the water. Then a voice whispered within my soul: "My son, I permitted you to go through the years of agony and pain that you might more fully witness of me to my young people. They stand today where you stood many years ago. They will listen to you, for you have been down those roads . . . and back. Can you not trust me, and tell others? I died for you. Will you not live for me?"

Once again the little spot was silent. I raised my face to the sky, visible through the lacy tree branches, and a feeling of determination filled my entire being. I recalled the faces of Jim, Sally, Joe, Pete, the others. In them had been recognition of the light of truth, granted by the Spirit of God.

"I'm ready, Lord," I whispered. "I'll fight back the pain and sickness I feel when I remember the loneliness and sinfulness of those years. No matter what it costs, I'll stand by your power as a living witness and glorify you. I'll speak to others that they might be spared what I have gone through...."

And in that moment I knew my quest to be a companion of God had ended.... My quest for souls had just begun.